THE LITTLE BLACK BOOK OF BUSINESS WRITING

MARK TREDINNICK is an award-winning poet, essayist, critic and writing teacher. His books include *The Little Red Writing Book* (reprinted four times and published in the United Kingdom and the United States as *Writing Well*), *The Little Green Grammar Book*, *The Land's Wild Music* and *A Place on Earth*, an anthology of Australian and US nature writing. His landscape memoir *The Blue Plateau* was published in 2009.

GEOFF WHYTE is a writer, editor and manuscript assessor. Following a brief detour into the field of education after completing a postgraduate diploma, Geoff established his business Whyte ink in 2005, providing editing at all levels and manuscript assessments.

THE LITTLE BLACK BOOK OF BUSINESS WRITING

Mark Tredinnick and Geoff Whyte

For Lesley, Maree and Pip, three muses
– Mark

For Margaret
– Geoff

A UNSW Press book

Published by
University of New South Wales Press Ltd
University of New South Wales
Sydney NSW 2052
AUSTRALIA
www.unswpress.com.au

First published 2010

10 9 8 7 6 5 4 3 2 1

National Library of Australia
Cataloguing-in-Publication entry
Author: Tredinnick, Mark.
Title: The little black book of business writing/Mark Tredinnick, Geoff Whyte.
ISBN: 978 174223 006 1 (pbk.)
Notes: Includes index.
Bibliography.
Subjects: Business writing – Handbooks, manuals, etc.
Other Authors/Contributors: Whyte, Geoff.
Dewey Number: 808.06665

Design Di Quick
Printer Ligare

This book is printed on paper using fibre supplied from plantation or sustainably managed forests.

CONTENTS

THANKYOUS

Mark would like to thank his wife, Maree, and Geoff would like to thank his partner, Margaret, for overseeing everything we overlooked at home while we wrote this book.

Thanks, above all, to our publisher, Phillipa McGuinness—for your encouragement, belief, patience and deft goading. Thanks, Pip. For their habitual professionalism, care and discipline, we're grateful to Heather Cam, Lauren Crozier, Chantal Gibbs, Matt Howard, Rosie Marson, Di Quick and Melita Rogowsky at UNSW Press, along with Jane Kembrey and the sales team. Thanks to our editor Stephen Roche for saving us from ourselves; and to our indexer Fiona Sim.

Trish Carroll of GALT Advisory helped with bright ideas, enthusiasm and examples. Professor Stan Glaser of the University of Western Sydney—fierce foe of management cant—helped in those ways, too. So did David Morris of Morris & Partners; he also led to Jack Vaughan, master copywriter. Thank you, Jack, for the use of some of your words. And Charles Dawson pointed us to the New Zealand awards for plain English, where we found some nice examples of clear and humane professional prose.

Thanks (from Mark) to my new old friend Anne Rimer—for the conversation, inspiration and accommodation. Not to mention the clippings. And speaking of clippings, thanks to Matt Gibbs for the care you take with the language of the Bard—and for the loan of the best ideas in this book. Michelle Willoughby of the Australian Catholic University, a smart writer herself, has been a generous reader and advocate of our work. And thanks to Donna Ward, who likes indigo better than black, but who helped nonetheless.

Thank you to everyone whose writing we have borrowed, reworked and critiqued in this book—those we acknowledge by name and those we don't. Thanks, especially, to clients. In particular, we'd like to acknowledge Juliet Lum and Cynthia Webster and Mark's erstwhile colleagues in the Faculty of Business and Economics at Macquarie University; and Kaaren Sutcliffe and others at the Australian National Audit Office.

Mark has been running business-writing workshops since 1996. Thanks to Jacqui Dent, Anne Maree Britton, Jonathan Saurine, John Jenkins and others who've helped, and to all the students who've come along.

Finally, Mark wants to express his gratitude to his friend and colleague Lesley Evans Nelson. You've been there from the start. You've listened, inspired, and carried the can, Lesley. So, thanks.

PROLOGUE: GOOD WRITING HABITS AND HOW TO GET THEM

Writing at work—there's just no escaping it

Far more of us write than ever wrote before, and too few of us know what we're doing.

The larger part of most people's work is writing: emails, letters, reports, contracts, tenders, proposals, responses to tenders, minutes, newsletters, media releases, marketing copy, presentations, applications, sales pitches, resignation letters. The works. At any given moment at work, you're more likely to be doing what we're doing now—trying to make sense with your fingers on a keyboard—than just about anything else. Writing is most of our work.

But in the same era when we've sat everyone in front of a computer and asked them to write for their keep, we've stopped teaching them anything much about composition, grammar and style. That equation comes out about the way you'd expect, and what it adds up to is not especially pretty writing. You get this, for example:

> For each parcel of land existing and future needs in regards to local open space, specifically assessing population projections, demographics and proximity to other public spaces is considered.

> Refugee and humanitarian clients bring their own challenges ... Many do not possess any proof-of-identity documentation and the majority are displaced to outside their country of origin.

> On the question as to whether the research 'will be of any practical use' by respondent DE 123 the case with real frozen corn supply is a clear example of practical use which was a real world problem raised by a frozen good firm.

> The organisational change programme will address the people, process and technology aspects required to support the department's communication vision.

> It is unlikely that any progress will emerge from the Major Economies Forum (MEF) by way of detailed programmatic specificity.

> The government is committed to supplying extra resource in support of this function.

On top of the fact that they've stopped teaching the young how to write, there's this: most people don't have much feeling for it, much love for it or, let's face it, much actual talent. Some people, hard though this is to believe, didn't pay much attention in English. Some people, apparently, looked out the window. Some found more magic in Pythagoras than Shakespeare. Most of us—we business executives, sales representatives, safety officers, engineers, lawyers, accountants, financial advisers, researchers, regulators, scientists, scholars and public servants—would rather do any number of other things than write. Many of us got into the line of work we pursue in part to avoid sentences and all the rest of it. But here we all are, nonetheless, writing our business lives away.

There's no escaping it: writing is a sentence we all have to serve. So we may as well serve it well. And the good news is it's never too late to learn.

If no one tells you how to write at work, you'll probably copy someone else. Which will be fine if they know what they're doing; if they know more about it than you do. Which they probably don't. They probably copied enough to stay alive from someone else, who probably copied … And so it goes. You get the picture. Copying will work fine for a busy writer at work, if you can tell what's worth copying from what's not, and most of us probably can't. But this book should help you.

This is a book of good habits to get, bad habits to lose and good copy to copy. It's *The Joy of Sex* for functional writers. We're writing it to make life easier for everyone who has to write at work; we're writing it to improve the quality of life of everyone, including ourselves, who has to read the stuff that passes for writing that comes their way from businesses and governments, schools, hospitals and just about everywhere else, by every conceivable medium, these days.

This book follows Mark Tredinnick's books *The Little Red Writing Book* and *The Little Green Grammar Book*, and it draws on them. *The Little Red Writing Book* is for everyone who wants to write—people for whom writing is an end in itself, as well as those with a purpose beyond writing in mind when they sit to write. But, in particular, it's for the poets, memoirists, essayists, novelists, professional writers and student writers among us. *The Little Green Grammar Book* is about the inner life of sentences; it looks at the nuts and bolts of writing; it's a grammar for everyone. Now, *The Little Black Book of Business Writing* targets the special needs of writers for whom the point *is* the point—people writing at work; people for whom writing is a core business function. We don't want to repeat too much of what Mark said in those books, so we'll cross-reference them quite often. This book can be as short as it is because those books precede it and deal with many points of style (abstraction and passivity, for instance) and syntax we would otherwise have to elaborate on here.

This book shows you how to write anything at work.

Every business document—every piece of every document, except the numbers, the illustrations and the graphs—is a piece of writing, and no matter how different each one feels, the same writing principles apply. So we begin, in the first three chapters, with a crash course in the aesthetics and methods of business writing.

Chapter 1 introduces the principles that apply to all functional prose, whatever the medium, message and market: write like you talk, only better; say nothing other than what you mean; spend words like scarce and pricey resources; use your writing to get your business done (not just to sound businesslike); manage writing like a project (whose purpose is to make sense and make the sale); take the time and trouble to save your reader time and trouble; above all, be clear. The chapter acknowledges the realities of business life that make functional writing hard to perform with grace—in particular, widespread institutional dedication to polysyllables and false elegance; the unforgiving pace of commerce; and the fact that most documents are written by many hands and need to pass through many levels of oversight. But, by means of examples of limpid financial, political, academic, scientific, bureaucratic and commercial prose, the chapter shows you how clarity, grace and economy are still possible at work.

Chapter 2 offers up twelve big—and enormously useful—ideas to help you improve your business writing; if you can count to twelve, you'll find most of your answers here.

Chapter 3 names the seven deadly sins that corrupt much business writing and make reading of it such a purgatory; then it lists the seven virtues, practising which you can redeem your writing and spare all of us who read you the particular torments of dysfunctional prose.

These three chapters lay down the law; they are the Vedas, the Dhammapada, the Beatitudes, the Commandments. We write them with love and care, because nothing in the book is more important or practical. They are also flush with examples of writing that cuts it and writing that doesn't—and the reasons why, and why not. Jump to the working chapters, if you like; but a fair bit of what we hope this book will teach, it teaches in these first three chapters.

In chapter 4, we look clinically at twelve varieties of document most commonly used in work environments. We don't cover every species of functional prose: there are too many variations, many of them narrowly adapted to particular business environments, and we have too little space to do them justice. In any event, most are variations of common themes, and it is those common themes we cover.

We don't lay out templates—again, we have too little space, and there are other books that do that. But this is not a book of precedents and boilerplates because we don't believe in templates. We believe in writing from scratch, most of the time, guided by robust first principles. Good writing sounds like it's been written just this once and just for the reader; and the best way to make it sound like that is to do it like that. We understand, of course, the efficiencies organisations are hoping for from templates and mandated phrasing, and they have their place. Where one uses them, they ought to be the very best writing the organisation ever does: vivid, trim, compelling and clear. But in truth the ideas that give rise to mandatory phrasing and dependence on templates—notions of conformity and control, the stifling of individual voices, the discouragement of originality and independent thought—are the chief cause of most of what is wrong with business writing in the first place.

So we won't be offering off-the-shelf documents here. Templating is the problem to which good writing is the solution.

All the same, there are documents you get to write quite often, and although writing goes best if you write those documents from scratch each time, it's helpful to develop some neat fixes to the openings, closings and transitions, for instance—elements of a letter or report you have to write each time. There are some tricks and techniques a writer can learn to help them improve their emails, letters, reports and other documents. In chapter 4, after outlining a model to help you write every business document more neatly, we workshop a selection of the documents most commonly encountered at work:

- letters
- emails
- reports
- executive summaries
- website copy
- minutes
- media releases
- newsletters
- job applications and resumés
- proposals
- instructional writing
- speeches.

In chapter 5, we answer some frequently asked questions—and a bunch of other questions that should, frankly, be asked more frequently. This chapter dispenses tips and take-home messages on

- dot points and how to keep them in their box
- graphs, charts, tables and figures
- good headings and bad headings
- corporate clichés
- business faux pas
- starting well

- finishing well
- attaching files
- fooling yourself into writing better
- getting yourself ready to write—planning and mapping
- the deft use of the first-person personal pronoun (*I*)
- abbreviations and how to spell most of them out
- when to capitalise, and how to do it sparingly
- the magic of verbs
- writing by ear
- earning your conclusions
- avoiding apostrophe catastrophes
- the art of the good word.

We close, in chapter 6, by making the case for elegance and economy, grace and style in business writing—the business case, the aesthetic case, the moral case, the political case, but above all, perhaps, the leadership case. Good writing—its care, its empathy, its clarity, its humanity, its beauty, its gift for listening and for telling the story, its power to inspire change—is a metaphor for leadership: for what it is, and what it takes. But more than a metaphor, good writing is a large part of what leadership entails; it is an important part of what leaders do. If you want to lead, if you want to make a difference, you're going to need to write well. Writing well has a way of making you attend more closely to what counts—a trick that leaders will need to master.

CHAPTER 1

WRITE AS IF YOU MEAN BUSINESS

The *business* of writing

In this book *business writing* includes all kinds of functional writing. By *functional writing* we mean writing that isn't written as literature. Creative writing may, among other things, inform its readers, but it is *art* performed with words, and it aims to work the way art (or entertainment) works. What it has to tell us is much less significant than how; in creative writing, the journey's the thing. In functional writing, the point is altogether the point. The function of the writing is to inform someone of something. It won't help to bore or confuse or annoy your reader. The language you want is practical, not artistic. It follows that anything you do with language in a functional setting that doesn't help to make the message clear is a thing you should stop doing.

While *business writing* appears in the title of this book, and while we use the phrase often in the text, we mean by it all categories of functional writing, every kind of writing in every line of work: in commerce, government, education, research, law, science, health, defence, the media, and so on. *Business writing* (and *work-based writing* and *functional prose*, and all the other synonymous phrases we employ) means the prose you make for work purposes. If you write at work, this book is for you, no matter what your work is.

Saving language from (bad) organisations and organisations from (bad) language

This little black book aims to dignify, democratise, trim and enliven the prose we use to govern ourselves and transact the greater part of our lives. We're writing this book to save language from organisations, and to save organisations (and the rest of us) from the kind of language those organisations, and the people they employ, seem to believe they have to write—language leached, it often seems, of anything much like sense or humanity. As here:

> Subsequent to the NAO audit, the Joint Committee of Public Accounts and Audit (JCPAA) undertook an inquiry into the National Health Scheme (NHS) Customer Feedback Systems series of audits. The JCPAA made a further three recommendations relating to complaints handling aimed at improving customer access on the NHS website.
>
> The reorganisation involved a move away from variable State based practices and the expansion of geographically dispersed teams resourced along national business lines.

Value-added writing

Business is fond of pet words, phrases and acronyms, some more replete with meaning than others: *KPI*, *ROI*, *QA*, *risk management*, *project management*, *value-adding*, *key drivers*, *initiatives*, *maximisation*, *key learning outcomes*, *going forward* ... Such words and phrases are conventional and seductive—and you'd have to say many writers in business and the wider diaspora of management-speak are, indeed, addicted to them. This addiction—the unreflective conformity with a slim lexicon of business (academic, bureaucratic, professional, management) words and phrases—causes most of the atrocities, fatuities and false economies of functional writing. And the truth is, you can do without all of them, and it will help; some of them, admittedly, are cute, but some are gross or plain silly, and none is compulsory.

But some business turns of phrase have some wisdom to share about business practice, if you stop long enough to let their meaning register. *Stakeholder value*, *return on investment (ROI)*, *productivity*, *benchmarking*, *cost–benefit*, *risk management*, *project management*, *sustainability*, *total quality management*, *client orientation*, *Pareto principle*, *deliverables*: all these, as long as you know (and let on) what you mean by them, are handy bits of language.

If they're worth using in business, these measures might be worth applying to *writing* in business, since writing is a central business process. Why do so few of us run productivity measures on, set key performance indicators for, wonder about the return we and our readers might receive on the investment of time and effort we make in, test the client orientation of, and insist on giving value to our stakeholders from, that key deliverable—business writing? Since we spend so much time doing it, and since so much organisational activity is transacted in words, it would make sense to treat writing as a core activity, a vital business process, and a key product. And it would make sense to audit, analyse, benchmark and workshop our writing, applying to our business communication the concepts that we say we value in other areas of organisational activity.

How efficiently do you write at work and how efficiently does your writing do what it's meant to do? How much meaning do you make, how much business do you do, how clearly, how swiftly, per syllable? How could you lift your game—how many empty, airy polysyllabic bits of jargon could you make redundant, for instance? What kind of return do you get (how often do you win the tender?), and what kind of return do you give (how much sense do you make?), from the valuable time and intellectual resources you invest writing proposals? How could you improve your returns, and the returns your readers get? What kind of value—measured as meaning per syllable, per sentence, per page; measured by the ease with which your stakeholders can fathom from your writing what you are doing and why; measured by how beautifully plain your documents are; measured by how well the writing of your prospectus keeps you out of court while also attracting investors—does your writing return to your enterprise's stakeholders? If you wrote better, would your enterprise do better business, would its stocks rise, would its customers be happier? Do you manage your writing as a project, and do you manage it with the same rigour you use on other projects? And if not, why not? What is your system for assuring the quality of your firm's writing? What does writing quality consist of, and how do you measure it and sustain it? Against what standards and exemplars do you benchmark your writing? The world's clearest? Or some murkier mark? And who is charged with assuring compliance with that standard? Do you pursue best practice at the keyboard—and how does that go again, and how do you roll it out across the organisation? Or is near enough good enough? What risks does your writing run—saying the wrong thing, saying nothing at all and taking a long time to say it, disappointing your readers' expectations that you will tell them something meaningful at a decent clip, for instance—and how are you managing those risks?

These are questions business people should ask of their writing, as they ask them of their other processes and assets. These are questions this book aims to help you answer. There are systems you could put in place. The *learning organisation* was only the start: you could become a *writing organisation*—one that places a high value on its writing, not just as outputs and deliverables, but as a way of thinking straighter and doing business with more grace and nous.

The head of human resources of a client of ours, a leading IT consultancy, contacted us recently in alarm. He'd worked out the reason why, despite the wonderful conditions they were in a position to offer, they were having trouble closing the deal with bright young IT graduates they hoped to employ: the length, density and legalistic language of the letter of offer, and the accompanying employment agreement, were frightening people off. The pomp and technicality of the way the letter was written represented the consultancy and its managers as pedantic and overbearing—troubling the prospective employees, who, in their interviews, would have encountered the same personable managers we knew. Apart from the inherent awkwardness and defensiveness of the writing, its tone was so out of keeping with that of the people the prospective recruits had met that many must have wondered if they were dealing with a kind of corporate bipolarity.

Our client had made a common mistake—privileging exactness over humanity, and in the process engendering mistrust. Most of the provisos and recitals and exceptions and references to industrial law made sense, though not all of them belonged in a letter of offer. Under the influence, presumably, of their lawyers, they had let themselves be so discriminating and cautious that they had found no room to sound like the kind of people anyone would actually want to work for. We managed to put the writing back into the humane and careful lingo the firm's people used in person, and in the process trimmed the document to half its length. Then the global financial crisis struck, and we're not in a position to say if our work did them any good. Nonetheless, the original document stands as an example of an investment in writing that did not produce happy returns; as an exercise in risk management that had failed to take account of the chief risk—that the offeree would be frightened off by the writing in which the offer was made.

Use writing to do business—not to sound like you're doing business

If we could offer just one piece of advice to writers, in universities, schools, banks, lawyers' offices, government departments, it would be this: don't use writing to *sound like* someone doing business (or policy or research or whatever); use writing to *do* business.

In other words, don't use language to sound like someone who knows what they're talking about; know what you're talking about, and use language to get it said. Let the writing disappear; let the message stand there plain; let the deal be done. The point isn't to sound like a bureaucrat, a business executive, a doctor, an accountant, an academic or a lawyer. The point is to be one and use your writing to get your work done.

Here is what a professor of accounting sounds like, who's less concerned with sounding *like* a professor of accounting than with making good sense (and perhaps also winning a grant) *as* a professor of accounting.

> This project tackles one of the major financial problems of recent times—how to better measure the risk of bankruptcy.

Here's how a Nobel laureate in economics writes about the global financial crisis in one of the leading intellectual journals in the world.

> No one can possibly know how long the current recession will last or how deep it will go.

Here's how a leading organisational theorist introduces a new idea in a classic management textbook.

> Let's think about organizations as if they were organisms.

Here's Charles Darwin, father of modern science, scrupulous practitioner of scientific method, writing up some science, way back in the days when we like to imagine writers were terribly stuffy.

> But this theory can be tested by experiment. Following the example of Mr Tegetmeier, I separated two combs, and put between them a long, thick, rectangular strip of wax: the bees instantly began to excavate minute circular pits in it.

Here's a politician addressing the incredibly complex and politically fraught issue of emissions trading schemes and the economics of other policy responses to global warming.

> So if we rule out an ETS (Emissions Trading Scheme) or a tax what are we left with? We could pass regulations to require power stations to clean up their act or use more renewable energy (that is what the Renewable Energy Target does now). This increases the cost of power and so electricity prices go up.
>
> We could pass regulations to make farmers plant more trees and change the way they manage their land. That increases the cost of food and fibre.
>
> Whichever way you look at it, going green is going to cost money and the challenge for any alternative policies to an ETS is to demonstrate that it will deliver lower cost abatement.

Here's a financial bureaucrat making sense and making us feel like she's a pretty cool and intelligent bureaucrat.

> With economic prospects improving, people's thoughts naturally turn to the question 'what next for monetary policy?' Financial markets were the first to ask this question. Virtually as soon as the cash rate stopped falling, the pundits started to speculate about the timing of the first increase.

Here's a lawyer finding a way to address her client's needs.

> The next step you'll need to take to advance your visa application is to have a health assessment. Your doctor should know what's required, but, just in case, take along the attached form with you. If you take the examination in the next two weeks, it will help us keep your application on track.

Here's an IT consultant making reasonable sense reasonably fast in a report to a prospect.

> This document outlines the IT design we developed for Northwest Oil out of the design workshops we ran with you recently.

Even the odd accountant finds a way, now and then, to demystify a complicated bureaucratic process.

> You'll need to complete this form and return it to us. As I understand the process, you'll also need to apply for an individual tax identification number (ITIN); you do this by submitting a form W-7, which I have also attached, along with instructions for filling it out.

Finally, here's a software company describing the function of some sensitive software on their entertainment products.

> 'Family Settings' is built into every Xbox 360. The program appears the first time you turn on your console, and you can access it via a password whenever you like after that. It allows parents to decide the kinds of games and movies family members can play or view.

Tell the story of the facts, and keep the story short. Say what you've found or announce what you're going to do, or pose the question you want to ask and get on with it. Awkwardness is not required. Nor is stiff formality.

The ultimate professionalism is to make sense fast, and to make sense pleasingly. It is to make elegant and economical sense of something your reader knows less about than you do; it is to make the complex beautifully simple; it is to talk intelligently and carry your reader with you to the end of the paragraph, to the end of the document, to a shared understanding, to agreement, to a sale, to whatever you're aiming at.

Taking a long time to make it short

Two things, at least, are true of business prose, and it pays to remember them well at the keyboard.

1. There isn't a person alive who wants to take a second longer than they must to *read* your email or your letter, your brochure or your report, your tender, your paper or your thesis.
2. There's not a person alive who wants to take a second longer than they must to *write* a work document.

Though we'd love to help you write faster, we'd rather help you write better. Writing better means helping your reader make sense fast: that's the speed that counts. In fact, most business writers need to learn the art of slowness. Slow down; work out what you're trying to say. Not something like it, but the thing itself in your own words. Now say it, putting all other ideas out of your head, dropping all the usual claptrap. Watch your reader get it fast: there's the speed you need.

The slower you write the thing in the first place, the faster and smoother it goes in the long run. The more care you take saying exactly and very clearly what you mean, without scaring your reader away or throwing them off the scent with unwarranted formality and obfuscation, the fewer bushfires you are likely to have to spend time putting out down the track—outbreaks of confusion and disaffection, not to mention litigation, caused by your initial haste.

This book shows you how to have your reader read your writing once and get it. Even love it. Concentrate on that. The better you learn these forgotten arts, the better you'll end up writing. Maybe even faster in the end.

Okay, so there's no Nobel Prize for business writing

Now, there's something we need to tell you: one of us is a poet. A poet cares for language the way business cares for profits, the way that science cares for methodological rigour, the way that law is said to care for justice. Well, the poet cares for all those things, too, but above all for the virtue and beauty and functionality of words and phrases, clauses and sentences and the music and meaning they make and the imagery they fashion along the way. For the rhythmic and linguistic art you can make with this rough vessel, speech.

And what poetry has to teach a functional writer is *care with words*. Poets these days tend to be poor; words are close to all they have, and so they like to spend them thriftily. Organisations would do well to treat words with the same kind of respect—as a scarce resource. Like a poet, they'd do well to waste none, to measure how much meaning they make per syllable they spend.

The poet should not offer even a single phrase to a reader that isn't, itself, a poem—a remarkable thing, a memorable utterance, fashioned not just for sense but for beauty. A poem must one way or another be beautiful. It must mean something, yes; but, more importantly, it must *be* something astonishing.

Above all, the letter or report, the email or contract, must *mean* something; and since time is short for all concerned, it may as well mean something fast. It works if it has something to say and says it, not just something like it. Clarity is the point in functional prose; form must serve function. The beautiful business document is the one that makes perfect sense; it disappears, leaving meaning—not bafflement, or mystery, or fury—behind it. Functional writing works, in other words, when it has a point and makes it, unambiguously—when it comes to that point fast and sticks with it to the end, and then stops.

There is no Nobel Prize for business writing. Matthew Gibbs, who writes elegant letters to the paper, smart sports journalism and trim financial media releases, likes to remind us of this whenever he thinks we're getting carried away with the aesthetics of functional prose. We remind him that one of the writers, Robert Solow, whom we quoted just now on the GFC, is a Nobel laureate; but it does us no good. It was for economics, not for literature, it was for his intellectual not his literary contribution that Solow, notwithstanding the elegance of his prose, won the Nobel. There's no Nobel Prize for business writing, Gibbs reminds us.

And he's right. Poetry is art; business writing is not. Business writing is functional, and its function is to tell us something. That doesn't mean it has to be deadly, as it so often is—or dull, at best, or evasive, ramshackle, awkward, stiff, prolix, Byzantine and pompous. It pleases us best when it says what it means in so many words. But if there were a prize, it would reward writing like Matthew's, in which the words never get in the way of the sense they're meant to make. Writing like this.

> John Maynard Keynes is in constant danger of giving the dismal science a good name. Keynes was indeed a renaissance man and a great friend of the arts. He was also something of a philosopher who warned against the pursuit of growth for its own sake instead of as a means to achieve a better life. If, thanks to the GFC, we're not all Keynesians already, we should be.

> With six of the top-10 selling books in Australia last year being for young people, children's literacy seems in good shape. But with four of the six being about teenage vampires, could the same be said about their dental health?

> If the first step along the path to redemption is to confess, here goes: I am a clipper. Not in the toenails, sailing ships or clasping sense, but with newspapers. I confess to being a butcher of broadsheets. I read a newspaper with a pair of eyes and a pair of scissors, ready to snip out items of interest.

> I chop up newspapers because I love them. To celebrate my recent birthday, some friends presented me with a pair of scissors, and a card, inscribed: 'Here's to 40 more wonderful years of clipping.' I was overwhelmed. Nearly decapitated. The oversized implements, the size of a golf club, would have intimidated Edward Scissorhands. I'm sure they breach new anti-terrorism laws.

That's how he writes at home; here's how he writes at work.

> ASX believes the timeframe and next steps outlined by the Government are appropriate, and will work constructively with the Government and ASIC to implement the transfer of responsibilities.

Okay, it doesn't zip so sweetly, but it's circumspect and trim enough. By contrast, for example, with the way most of his colleagues in the regulatory and financial worlds might have turned it out.

> It is our considered view that the benchmarks signalled by the Government going forward are fair and reasonable, and we are committed to working constructively with all parties involved to facilitate implementation of the reframed accountability paradigm in a timely manner.

The only prize the business writer wants is the business her writing sought: the job, the gig, the contract, the attention and admiration of her audience, the getting or the avoiding of a headline. Writing is meant to help you get the business done. The business writer uses the words to get her where she means to get, and only there, and nowhere else, and, with any luck, fast.

A workshop participant once said that what he wanted above all to learn from the workshop was how to keep a client reading beyond his second paragraph. He wanted, like all writers, to be heard, to feel he had not wasted his time or his client's, and to see his writing fulfil its purpose—which was to say what he meant it to say. And to win, as a consequence, the contract.

Business is a true story you wage with words

Business might be measured in money, but it's transacted in language; we may weigh it in numbers, but we wage it in words.

We do business, if we have any choice in the matter, with those people who convince us they can give us what we need the way we want to get it. Oh, there's the question of price, of course, but that doesn't come into it until we hear and assess the story. You want the work—you make the pitch, you make yourself stand out, and you make your firm irresistible. You want the world to hear about your research, and you want them to put it into practice—you tell what you've found as a story the world is going to want to read and never going to want to forget. You want to get the degree—you do the research and you write it up as a thesis. You want to win the case—you have to make the argument, and you have to make it stick. You want the world to buy your product, you want the client to use your services—you have to turn what you do into a sound bite or two and get it out there.

You have to make a story out of the numbers and the technicalities and the operations and find the people who need to hear it, and tell it to them compellingly. You want the grant, you write the application; you want the government to change its mind, you write the letter; you want the agency to change course, you write the policy proposal; you attend the accident, you write the report; you see the patient, you write your notes. You write the strategic plan, the job ad, the job application, the mission statement, the marketing flyer, the media release, the email query, the audit report, the financial statement …

Each of these is a story. It's a case or a proposition, and you're going to need words to make it, and the better chosen your words and the greater impact they have, the more your story—which it is your business to tell—cuts through.

And this is real life here, so your story should be true; you'd better get the facts straight; you'd better not evade or dissemble or mumble abstractly in the usual polysyllabic mumbo-jumbo. But getting the thing straight and true is not where you stop; that's just where you start.

Beyond the primary objective of making sense, each business document has a purpose: to get the work, to make the sale, to win the case, to get the degree, to apologise and set things right, to meet the regulatory requirements, to inform the parliament and the people of Australia. And when you think about it from the reader's point of view—something more business writers should do more often—the document will find its target and deliver its payload of meaning faster and smoother, the easier the writing is to read, the more transparently and persuasively it makes its point, the less of its reader's time it wastes. The more economical and lucid the writing is, the more it positions its author as someone we believe and feel we'd like to deal with.

And you must tell your story in your own language. It sounds false otherwise. If you want to tell your truth, if you want to get the gig, you're going to need to do more than tell your story in your best imitation of the language you think you're obliged to use. A writer is not a ventriloquist's dummy. You'll want your writing to stand out—as readable, at very least (for most functional writing is not very readable, and it will help you if yours is); or even, as breathtakingly clear.

In cases where you're writing to pitch for work, to win a tender or a job, you might want your writing to do more than stumble towards its point; you might want it to speak of your intelligence, perspicacity and acuity. You might want to use it to make yourself sound like more than your average drone; you might want to sound like someone like yourself. Using the same turns of phrase, the same clichés, as everyone else will make you sound like everyone else. Which might be good enough for some writing and some writers some of the time. But it's never compulsory; if sometimes it's necessary, it's hardly ever sufficient. Which is to say, good writing always has some character. It has voice. If you think it helps to put your readers to sleep, go ahead and sound like no one; go ahead and copy the idiom. If you'd like them to stay awake, try writing that sounds like a tidied kind of talking. Especially if it's you you're talking about.

You'll never write alone

Poets write alone. It's how it has to be. But if you're writing at work, you'll be writing in company. The academic has a co-author; the public servant has a thousand bosses (each draft usually has to pass up through four or five levels of oversight); the marketing executive has to get her boss to sign off the media release before it goes out. Emma Tennant once—bitterly—defined the editor as 'the complete stranger who rewrites your copy to suit his or her own ideas and changes the position of every comma'. That gets close to a job description of many bosses. Alas.

Because of the nature of organisations, you rarely, if ever, write alone; you speak for the whole mob and its products, not just for yourself. The author must surrender some of their *author*ity. It's the deal we sign up to, in return for which we draw a salary.

But writing is hard enough with one pair of hands on the keyboard; it's hell with seven. And it tends not to improve the prose. It is, nonetheless, what most writers have to deal with at work. We need to concede this at the outset. Voice and elegance are hard to maintain when every manager whose desk your writing crosses opens Track Changes and makes 'improvements'. So, how do you write well under these circumstances? Manage your expectations and do your best within them: get your syntax straight; get your facts straighter; trim excesses of every kind. Make yourself a small target, in other words. But never surrender your authority. If you're charged with the writing, *write* it and never stop. Pass it up the line; argue for clarity you think is being compromised; give in where you have to; don't let anyone else rewrite it—that's always your job. Manage up; defend the writing. But not for your ego's sake—for the reader's sake, for the sake of the message and the organisation's brand and the integrity of the language itself.

Manage up; never *give* up. But also know that it's in the nature of things that you don't get to make all the decisions, and you probably won't win every fight. Learn to argue winningly for your prose; learn as much as you can about your prose, so you can do that with reference not just to your personal opinion, but to higher authorities; learn to bargain and consult.

You might write the leanest, smartest, most clear-spoken report your department has ever written—exemplary in every way and consonant with your department's espoused values of plain English—but you still might find your report savaged at the top because you failed to take the man or woman at the top into the tent when the writing was going on. The politics of bureaucracies, schools and big corporations being what they are, good writing may need some shepherding through. Politics kills clarity; but clarity may need some politics to help it cut through.

Feel the fear and write it anyway

Writing at work is too often performed as an act of conformity with a narrow rubric of usages—a template of polysyllabic words, phrases and sentences, like this:

> We can see an emergence of organic synergy, going forward. At this point in time, we remain committed to embedding exampling into the existing textual construct to facilitate ongoing sustainability.

This writing is absurd; it doesn't go the way writing is meant to go. Writing is transcribed and tidied speech; writing is talking on paper; and it goes best, and says the most, the most smoothly, when it goes the way good talking goes—when it sounds like an accomplished kind of conversation.

The kind of writing we just sampled doesn't do what writing is meant to do—it doesn't speak; and it doesn't really mean. It fails in large part because it has none of the vernacular music of speech, and of transcribed speech—writing. As readers, in spite of so much writing that fails to deliver, we tune in to writing, expecting it to say something meaningful to us; we listen in expectation of a clear voice saying something. This is, above all, what readers—all readers, everywhere—want writing to do. So writing, in particular functional writing, should be a writer's best attempt to say—to *say* on paper, as though he or she were a real live human being talking intelligently with another—what he or she means. Too many writers and too many of their managers insist upon writing that barely deserves the name; and they do it, presumably, out of fear—fear of change, fear of sounding unbusinesslike or unprofessional, fear of making too much sense, fear of being different. It's got to be fear, the writing it produces is so fearful. Not to mention useless.

Too many writers lack the courage, the technique or the knowledge to challenge the template and *write*. But most of us mistrust and dislike longwinded, stuffy and evasive writing when we read it; the trick is to remember how little we like such writing when we write it ourselves. We need to resist convention and copy only the kind of writing that gives us, when we read, no struggle at all—the kind that sounds like accomplished talking. Remember this: there isn't a reader out there—there isn't a boss, there isn't an academic journal, there isn't a customer or a board member or an examiner of your thesis—who wants the kind of writing you, yourself, dislike. No one wants the reading to be hard work; no one wants to struggle to work out what you mean; no one wants to read 170 pages in order to still be guessing what you're trying to (or, more likely, trying not to) say. Bank on it: everyone wants clarity; and the best way to be clear is to know what you're talking about—and then to talk it out on paper.

It doesn't want to sound like chatter; we're all too busy for that. And you're going to need some fancy terms and you're going to need to get them straight. It's okay to sound authoritative; but you're more likely to keep your reader with you all the way to the prize if you never stop sounding like you're in the room with them, at the top of your form, performing an accomplished kind of talking. Notice how this paragraph on a tricky subject does all that, favouring ordinary expressions ('agrees', 'while some commentators blame', 'as many countries look to adopt'). It sounds like good financial journalism; in fact, it's a paper by a young academic.

> The confluence of many factors brought about the recent global financial crisis. While some commentators blame the relaxed credit practices of banks, others have emphasised the use of fair value accounting (FVA) in financial reporting (Banziger, 2008; Deloitte, 2008). Those critics argue that, by veiling and often inflating the real value of key assets, FVA may have encouraged imprudent investing and so helped bring on and deepen the financial crisis that began with the bursting of the sub-prime bubble. This paper agrees with that conclusion and proposes amendments to the international standards to control for the risks associated with FVA; it argues that this is especially important and urgent right now, as many countries look to adopt international accounting standards in which FVA is entrenched.

Smarten it up, don't dumb it down

David Malouf once wished that more writing—of all kinds, especially the kind we have to read, as opposed to the kind we choose to read—were written in 'the intelligent vernacular'. That's the great Australian writer's elegant, slightly old-world way of saying like tidied speech: sophisticated in thought, elegant in construction, clear (like good talking) in expression. Simple, sound, smart, clear.

In his book on the writing craft, *Style: Toward Clarity and Grace*, Joseph Williams has pointed out that every culture of sophisticated men and women evolves a discourse of administration, management and politics as it grows more settled and 'civilised'. The diction of bureaucracy becomes more and more remote from the vernacular—from the language spoken on the streets and in the markets, written in the great books and spoken on the stage. The diction of administration is marked by certain qualities: studied impersonality, a focus on processes and abstractions, a calmness and authority of tone. Much of this character evolves out of the institutionalisation of certain social functions, the practices of governance, which leave the hands of people known to each other in communities and fall to formal entities. Some of the impersonality arises from the need many specialists feel to protect their special knowledge from abuse, theft or possibly even comprehension by the masses.

But the separation of the language of government and business from the language of the rest of life does not, on the whole, serve the public interest. It obscures the workings of government, business, education and the professions from the public. It mystifies what could be plain; it obscures what should—because liberty and livelihood depend on the sense this language is straining to make—be transparent.

But it's always been thus, and perhaps it always will be. The transparency of public office, the advancement of knowledge and the promotion of intelligent and inclusive democracy depend, though, upon bringing the vernacular and administrative languages back into conversation. The health and loveliness of the language depend upon that reconciliation too. We have a duty to the language, with which we make sense of the world, inside which we learned how things tick, to keep it lively and strong, to see it used honestly, carefully and freshly. Bureaucratic discourse and the unbeautiful cadences of business English attenuate the language rather than renewing it.

Another tradition—dedicated to the idea that one of the greatest public services an agency can deliver is to communicate clearly—has always worked within the system of governance we inherit, unravelling the convoluted syntax of public documents, weeding out the infestations of prickly and intractable clauses that keep breaking out, for instance, on the hills around the Parliamentary Triangle. This tradition has been championed for years in Australia by the editors at the Australian Government Publishing Service. In the last ten or fifteen years, in many countries including Australia, the ideals of plain English have become orthodox and almost universally accepted across government. Sometimes they're even put into practice.

The Institute of Public Administration Australia (IPAA) commented in the preamble to the judges' report for their annual report awards not all that long ago that 'all annual reports produced for government, at any level, should be clear, concise and accurate. They need to paint a full and complete picture of the agency, its work, and its contribution to the achievement of the goals of government.' By using both 'full' and 'complete', they show how much harder it is to practise than to preach plain English; still, their point is clear. If not concise—let alone trim. In their summary of assessment, the IPAA judges noted that all the winning reports were written in plain English.

Audit offices around the world report to the government and, beyond the government, to the people who elect it and pay the taxes that fund government agencies, how those agencies are performing their duties, and how, in particular, they are spending the money that funds them. More than is the case for other government documents, audit reports are meant to be written for the broader public, and audit offices in many parts of the world have led the way in promoting a prose style marked by elegance, transparency and clarity.

The *Style Guide* of the National Audit Office (UK) begins with these comments, which many public sector writers would do well to remember.

> [Audit reports] need to get their messages across clearly and simply to an audience who probably do not need or wish to know the details and complexities surrounding the subjects examined.
>
> Writing NAO reports is not so different from any other kind of

> informative writing. To give our readers a comfortable ride, use verbs actively, write short sentences and keep to the essentials.

They say, even before that

> Clear writing depends on clear thinking. To draft well a writer must know just what he wishes to convey. You can usually say what you mean in short, vigorous everyday words. This is especially important if you are writing about a complex subject. Readers will need all their attention to grasp what they are being told. They don't want to spend time grappling with obscure language as well.

In 1991, the Office of the Auditor General in Ottawa put together the agreements that resulted from a meeting of communication experts, legislators and auditors from many parts of the world, who had come together to talk about how to compose clear audit reports. That meeting concluded that the two most important characteristics of audit prose are these:

- using commonly understood language
- writing and designing for busy and impatient readers.

This second point emphasises the need for clear, simple and conspicuous structure in documents, clean layout and good graphics—as well as an accessible prose style.

Closely following these two characteristics (both of them reader-oriented) came another that is equally oriented to the needs of readers, not the constraints or habits of the writer:

- the writer needs to reward the reader's effort by making the reading experience efficient and engaging.

The conference concluded that these matters all come *ahead* of the other important factors:

- achieving accuracy, balance and fairness in reporting findings and making recommendations

- making it clear what the reader is meant to do next or what will happen next.

Thinking straight in plain language; organising your thought and designing your document to reveal (rather than hide) your message and the logic behind it; expressing yourself on all topics, especially those most likely to tax a reader, in everyday language; engaging your reader; keeping the writing trim; and rewarding a reader's attention by making the writing lucid and simple and easy to stay with—this is what public sector writers, and all other functional writers, should be doing. Accuracy, balance, fairness and utility—those much-vaunted qualities—are not really writing principles. They're vital, of course, but they're matters of governance and ethics, and if they're not being done, public service is not being performed. They're where we start—the sine qua non. Writing that's inaccurate, unbalanced, unfair and useless is hardly writing at all, anyway. But once the writing starts, if it's writing we're doing, let's make sure it's writing and not something else—spin, for example, or obfuscation, time-serving, or obscurantism or timid conformity.

What the audit bodies are describing so well is writing in the intelligent vernacular. People who are afraid—or unable—to make their writing simple, call it dumbing down. But if you think hard and speak it plain–it's smartening up.

Writing plainly demands discipline and care from writers at every level of the writing process: in *choosing words* (favouring the everyday and concrete over the technical and abstract); in *making sentences* (favouring the elegant and simple over the convoluted; favouring the active over the passive; favouring the human-centred over the process-oriented); in *shaping paragraphs* (favouring the deductive (starting with your conclusion and justifying it) over the inductive (closing with your conclusion); favouring the flowing over the chaotic); in *planning documents* (favouring a simple, clear design over a loose or complex one); and in *selecting content* (guarding against the inclusion of all but the most essential information and detail).

Work to make every word tell (as Strunk and White famously advised). Keep every word, phrase, sentence, paragraph and document apt, shapely, clear and alive. It's as simple—and as difficult—as that.

CHAPTER 2

TWELVE BIG IDEAS

1 There is no secret

Don't tell anyone, but business writing is the same as any other kind of writing, except it's about business.

Writing well at work demands the same kind of attention and uses the same kind of language as any other decent piece of writing—it employs the same diction, the same range of sentences, and it is precisely the same kind of exercise in sounding out meaning on paper. There is no special tone required; you don't have to talk in tongues. The only thing that distinguishes business or bureaucratic or academic or professional writing from any other kind of writing is what it's about.

Business writing is writing about business, for business purposes. It's just writing in a business context, so all the rules of grammar and style apply. As they do every time you pick up a pen. No one gets an exemption from making sense; clarity is not negotiable. Nor grammar, for that matter; nor economy. There's really only one style a writer—in business, in government, in education, in law, in science, you name it—wants to affect, and that's *good* style.

Good writing—about anything—will be clear, at least; at best, compelling. Writing runs off the rails at work when its authors affect a business or formal 'style'—favouring long, technical, abstract words and awkward phrasing, stripping sentences of any kind of human life. Bad business writing is bad because it assumes there is a secret language and tries too hard to affect it.

> Respond to the 2008 Financial Crisis. Evolve [what—overnight?] to meet the new financial planning paradigm [which would be?]. Providing total returns [as opposed, one supposes, to partial returns], improved performance and control. For SMSF and HNW clients. Unique open ended flexibility.

> Those in control of the human resources capability sector are confronted with a decision-making process that involves accountability in implementation and must deliver positive outcomes in a leveraged manner.

> As part of ongoing initiatives to minimize costs and provide more efficient methods of communicating with our stakeholders, we are writing to encourage shareholders to provide their email addresses as the medium for future communications.

You'd expect Virgin's writing to capture the entrepreneurial spirit and youthful temperament of that group of companies. Yet this little piece of writing from one of their more enterprising sections falls flatter than it needs to because it overdoes the business-speak, as though it were de rigueur.

> Virgin Green Fund focuses on middle market growth and expansion investment opportunities in the renewable energy and resource efficiency sectors including water. Our objective is to help companies realize their full growth potential. We back strong management teams deploying field-proven technologies. Our team's operating, strategic and financial experience combined with our sector expertise and the breadth and strength of our networks contributes to achieving long-term value creation. Virgin Green Fund invests across stage, geography

> and technology in its core sectors. We provide equity to achieve a wide variety of objectives, including growth capital, management buyouts, recapitalizations and corporate spin-outs. Diversification and thoughtful portfolio construction are cornerstones of the Fund's approach.

An objective 'to help companies realize their full growth potential' is much blander than it needs to be and not really an accurate description of their objective at all; to get that you need to read all the other sentences. And the less said about 'invests across stage, geography and technology in its core sectors' the better. This copy, though competent, is a missed opportunity for leadership and competitive edge.

Sticking with Virgin for a minute, this copy from their group website does a better job of telling us who they really are.

> *We believe in making a difference.* Virgin stands for value for money, quality, innovation, fun and a sense of competitive challenge. We deliver a quality service by empowering our employees and we facilitate and monitor customer feedback to continually improve the customer's experience through innovation.
>
> When we start a new venture, we base it on hard research and analysis. Typically, we review the industry and put ourselves in the customer's shoes to see what could make it better. We ask fundamental questions: is this an opportunity for restructuring a market and creating competitive advantage? What are the competitors doing? Is the customer confused or badly served? Is this an opportunity for building the Virgin brand? Can we add value? Will it interact with our other businesses? Is there an appropriate trade-off between risk and reward?

If you know how to *talk well* about something, you know the only secret worth knowing about writing well at work: writing is talking transcribed, and it goes well when it sounds like someone who knows what they're talking about, talking to you intelligently about it. Like this, for instance.

> Global warming is caused by the massive increase of greenhouse gases, such as carbon dioxide, in the atmosphere, resulting from the burning

of fossil fuels and deforestation. There is clear evidence that we have already elevated concentrations of atmospheric carbon dioxide to their highest level for the last half million years and maybe even longer. Scientists believe that this is causing the Earth to warm faster than at any other time during, at the very least, the past one thousand years.

Aviation contributes two per cent of all man-made carbon dioxide emissions globally, and we acknowledge our contribution to global greenhouse gas emissions and are committed to being part of the climate change solution.

At BDW we treat others as we would wish to be treated ourselves: with honesty, fairness and respect.

The Australian National Audit Office (ANAO) is a specialist public sector practice providing a full range of audit services to the Parliament and Commonwealth public sector agencies and statutory bodies. Our audit clients include some 300 government bodies.

('Clients', just as an aside, has always seemed a linguistic stretch to us—since the 'government bodies', quite rightly, have hardly any say in whether they receive the 'service' or not, and since the real client, or at least the reader for whom the report is written, is the parliament and, by extension, us, the taxpayers, who pay for the service (and for the government bodies audited). The government body is the subject of the report, but not the client of the people who write it.)

But writing is not, in fact, talking. It works in literal silence. But when you write, you replicate on paper or on a screen—by forming up letters, and making words from them, and phrases from those, and clauses from those, sentences from them, paragraphs, chapters and so on—the sounds with which we make sense to each other when we open our mouths and talk. Writing is talking transcribed; no one understands a thing until they hear in their heads the sound patterns your writing makes. So—to summarise the idea that animates *The Little Red Writing Book*—if writing is talking on paper, it will go best when it sounds like talking. Writing doesn't need another set of words than talking; it doesn't need its own syntax; but it does need to be more carefully made. It isn't helpful, it isn't easy, and it simply isn't necessary to favour for the page words and structures you wouldn't use in speech. Use the everyday word ahead of the scientific or technical expression, George Orwell recommended in 'Politics and the English Language', way back in 1946, unless you want to contribute to the corruption of the language and make yourself look silly.

But because writing isn't *in fact* talking—it is, of course, silent talking transacted remotely on a screen or a sheet of paper—it needs to be tidier, and generally shorter, than talking. For a few reasons. First because, if you take away the non-verbals (the tone of voice, the raised brow, the crazy walk, the fancy tie, the talking hands, the banter), all you have are the words. They need to be that much more carefully chosen; they need to make sense without the aid of the gestures; and they need, if you are to keep your reader's attention and interest, to have about them the human qualities (voice, animation, character) that your speaking had (if it was any good), just because you were speaking it in company.

Second, the system by which we manufacture meaning on the page is slower and more convoluted, by its nature, than the conversational system we employ when we talk: writing takes longer for the writer to perform and longer for the reader to unpack than talking. So, each written word must give more value than each spoken word—or you start to lose your reader. Paradoxically, it is by making their writing trimmer on the page than it would be in speech that a writer allows their writing to work like—and sound like—speech. Making each word pull its weight, you compensate on paper for the absence of the non-verbals; you lend your prose the qualities of speech upon which rich and effective communication depends.

A simple recipe for working women who don't have a wife. Don't you wish you could come home from a day's work and be waited on? So does the rest of the family. But while you're waiting for a miracle, why not try a few Short Cuts. Short Cuts are easier, more efficient meat meals.

The policy tools exist to create the incentives required to change investment patterns and move the global economy onto a low-carbon path. This must go hand-in-hand with increased action to adapt to the impacts of the climate change that can no longer be avoided.

Welcome to HN, the country's leading retailer. We have all your electrical and computer needs covered ... We supply customers with quality products and professional service every day.

The Great Inflection is the mass diffusion of low-cost, high-powered innovation technologies—from hand-held computers to Web sites that offer any imaginable service—plus cheap connectivity. They are transforming how business is done.

The last few decades have belonged to a certain kind of person with a certain kind of mind—computer programmers who could crank code, lawyers who could craft contracts, MBAs who could crunch numbers. But the keys to the kingdom are changing hands.

Write like you're talking about something you know to someone you trust. (Even if you're not.)

Write like you speak, only better.

2 More care, less formality

Everybody insists that writing at work must be more formal than speaking and other forms of writing. Don't be fooled. Striving to affect whatever they think formality means, writers neglect two things of much more importance—clarity and the true courtesy of talking to your reader as though you respected their need to get your message easily—to the enterprise of writing. Attempting formality, most of us achieve pomposity.

> Data conversion is a crucial exercise and should provide an accurate benchmark to assist with the planning of the go live data conversion.
>
> Should timing change, project management effort will be adjusted accordingly.
>
> It was identified that staff throughout the organisation responsible raising requisitions for goods and services will be able submit requisitions via iPOS.
>
> The new Bulletins system was launched on 30 April 2010. This is information regarding how HO Underwriting will utilise the system to communicate changes. Previously, communications specific to the Regions were termed Circulars and those to Agents were Technical Bulletins. All information will now be issued via the system as Bulletins, so to differentiate between them for the purposes of explaining how the system will be used, we will refer to circulars as 'regional instructions' and Technical bulletins as 'general instructions'.
>
> It is anticipated that the group will be presented with a range of recommendations aimed at enhancing the effectiveness and efficiency of our operations going forward.

Have the courage and courtesy to write simply and without affectation. If formality means anything useful to a writer at all, it's that you take the trouble to do those things. When you write with care, 'formality' takes care of itself. The writer who cares enough—for language and for the organisation she represents and for her own reputation and, above all, for her reader—will write less formally than is normal, more plainly and simply. More like someone whose copy anyone would want to keep reading. More like someone you'd want to do business with. Good writing sounds like someone talking sense, with your interests, not just their organisation's, in mind. Good writing is the best conversation you never heard.

> I wanted to get back to you on the issues you raised at the training session last week.

> The other school of thought, which might be termed 'medical', advances the argument that placing a mental health unit within a general hospital, or on the hospital campus, reduces the stigma for patients; mental illness is treated like any other illness.

> Chapter two concludes with two recommendations for establishing risk-based evaluations of outlay programs.

It's cheating, of course, to use a piece of advertising copy from one of the great copywriters—copy concerning cognac, no less, and one of the great cognacs, at that. But it shows you how like one half, at least, of a good conversation great copy can be.

> Remy Martin Luis XIII Grande Champagne Cognac normally retails for $1500 a bottle. But that's not the surprise. The surprise is it doesn't cost more ... The condensate is poured into small *limousin* oak barrels made in Remy's own cooperage. No nails or glues are used—river reeds fill the gaps. Then, it's into the cool, dark tranquility of the *chais*, the earth-floored cellars hewn into the hillsides of Charentais stone. For no less than half a century. After which time, the cellarmaster (or more likely his son or grandson) will compose this symphony of cognac.

Some nice, plain geology now:

> In the late Cretaceous and early Tertiary time, mountains began to rise beneath the wide seas and marsh flats of Wyoming.

And a word or two from Google:

> In 2004, when Google founders Larry Page and Sergey Brin wrote to prospective shareholders about their vision for the company, they outlined a commitment to contribute significant resources, including one percent of Google's equity and profits in some form, as well as

> employee time, to address some of the world's most urgent problems. That commitment became Google.org. Google.org ... works closely with a broad range of 'Googlers' on projects that make the most of Google's strengths in technology and information; examples include Flu Trends, RechargeIT, Clean Energy 2030, and PowerMeter.

So here's another rule to guide your writing at work: write informally and carefully, not formally and carelessly. Disregard, respectfully, all the usual injunctions—you hear them daily pretty much everywhere (in the academic world, the public sector, in law and science, business and government)—to write formally. No jacket is required. Contractions are fine; so too, a little first person; and the short words are better than long ones almost every time.

'False elegance' is the polite name given to the kind of awkward pomp you get from the addiction to formality. Care is what we need. Careful, sophisticated, clear thinking; and astute word choice. There is no room for ambiguity or merely personal opinion. But no amount of passive voice ('it is recommended') and polysyllabic diction can manufacture objectivity or specificity—which are qualities of thought, not by-products of diction. Following Aristotle ('think like the wise man; express yourself like the common man'), Orwell (who insisted that functional writing favour the everyday expression over the technical and arcane) and others, the plain English movement has been arguing for careful informality since the late 1960s. Careful, circumspect informality is also what David Malouf means by the intelligent vernacular. It's what you want at work. More care; less formality.

3 Writing is branding

Most of us are familiar with the marketing concept of 'positioning'. By the way it turns its products out, how it prices, publicises and packages them, an organisation positions its goods or services—its 'deliverables'—

for the public. Products positioned to correspond to the needs of buyers are more likely to get bought.

But organisations attract and keep customers not only—not even mostly—by how aptly they position their products in the relevant market; organisations are positioning chiefly themselves. Through their products, their packaging, their advertising and their brand, they tell a story of who they are. If you find that story engaging—if you think this mob might be good to do business with—you're more likely to buy and keep buying.

How we write positions our message—more or less successfully. But it also brands us. It says something about who we are, what we value, how straight we think, how much trouble we take, how dependable we are.

How you write is who you are. So, who do you want to be? However that sounds is how you want to make your writing go.

How do you want to sound: pompous, lofty, hasty, prolix; blunt, rude, sloppy, self-important; conforming, evasive, muddle-headed, passive-aggressive; or, perhaps, lucid, relaxed, authoritative, respectful?

The hospital administrator who writes

> we just want to ensure that both hospitals are optimised

doesn't sound like he runs the kind of hospitals we'd like to be sick in. He makes us wonder what he isn't saying—what he really means.

And successful though the organisation is whose website says

> The primary objective of W-Corp is to provide a satisfactory return to its shareholders

their writing doesn't distinguish them at all. Their objective is, of course, in corporations theory and law, the purpose, or duty of every business enterprise. So that writing says nothing; and it positions them as unimaginative.

You feel like doing business with this crowd, though. They seem smart and relaxed.

> Most businesses recognise the importance of watching the numbers. But that's only half the picture. To achieve the right numbers first you need the right ideas. That's what we do … We find the right ideas for you and help you plan your investments around them.

Writing is branding: unless you want to sound like everyone else, don't write like everyone else thinks they're supposed to; write like yourself at your best on a very good day. Write to make yourself and your mob irresistible, smart, humane, original and real—or whatever adjectives you'd like your readers to attribute to you.

Here's how one airline you may have flown with positions themselves as the kind of employer you'd like to have.

> Make our flight path your career path. Whether aviation is your passion, you are looking for a successful and rewarding career, or you want to develop your skills and experience in a dynamic and challenging environment, there could be something great here for you.

Here's how the same airline handles baggage.

> You may take, free of charge, baggage weighing up to 7 kg on board with you, which might consist of: …

And here's the other mob.

> For the safety and comfort of all our customers, and to ensure compliance with Civil Aviation Safety Authority Regulations, it is necessary to limit the size, weight and number of each customer's carry-on baggage.

Then you have to wade through a further five paragraphs before you actually learn how much hand luggage you can carry on board. Not such a great exercise in branding as their competitor's.

4 Writing thrives when thinking thrives

Good equations are elegant; good thinking is sound and sharp; good athletes move only as many muscles about as much as they need to; the best businesses are efficient—they use scarce resources prudently. Things thrive when they're elegant—when they do as much as they need to—but no more. Good writing is like that, too. It uses as little language as it can to say just what it means in just the tone it means to.

In *The Little Red Writing Book*, Mark wrote about a student in a business writing workshop who said his father had always told him to aim at 'thrift' in his writing. 'Thrift' is the noun; 'thrive' the verb. When the writing is spare, when you say only and precisely what you mean in as few words as you can manage, your writing will thrive.

Writing thrives when thinking thrives—when thinking is allowed to operate free of claptrap and cant—and business prospers as a result.

Writing, at work especially, is like maths or science or business. It thrives when it's thrifty. With words. Writing works best when it's generous with the truth, but economical with how it tells it.

It is one of the contradictions of managerialism—an ideology that plays through government agencies, hospitals, prisons, universities and primary schools now, not just businesses—that it commits us all to effectiveness and efficiency while practising and promoting profligacy with words. It's wanton with words; it makes much more noise than sense.

The review of the performance of the Strategic Indigenous Housing and Infrastructure Program (SIHIP) noted, among other things,

> It is clear that in the development of the initial packages of works an imbalance emerged between program objectives. Elements such as design and community engagement were elevated to the detriment of the unit cost required to achieve program targets, thereby skewing program outcomes.

Contrast this with the clarity of thought and speech in the interim report of the 2009 Victorian Bushfires Royal Commission.

> From the evidence heard to date, the Commission believes that immediate changes are required to the State Emergency Response Plan (SERP). The SERP does not clearly designate the agency responsible for issuing warnings and recommending relocation.

Writing is thinking articulated—a matter of some concern, given some of the things that come across our desks. While there's no guarantee—especially these days when so many academics, bureaucrats and others seem addicted to strange and prolix idioms—that a clear thinker will write lucidly, this much is true: clarity in prose is impossible without clarity of thought. Writing can only thrive where thinking thrives. Work at it hard enough and your writing will school your thinking in clarity and soon enough improve your business.

Clarity, in prose of all kinds, sits next to godliness; you'll achieve it by practising thrift.

5 It's for the reader, stupid

Forget who's reading. Just remember *someone* is. A person like you: an intelligent grown-up in a hurry.

Concentrate on who's doing the *writing* (that would be you), and make the writing sound like the orderly speech of a person who knows what they're talking about. Write to sound like yourself at your best (speaking of something you know to someone you trust). Write to please yourself—as you like to be pleased when you have to read this kind of stuff. If you're anything like us, you'll want it clear and short and vivid and voiced. Make yourself, as William Faulkner once said, hard to please. As hard as you are to please as a reader.

But writing is, by nature, a practice of empathy. Good writing, anyway.

Writing is an abstracted conversation performed, admittedly, on paper (or a screen) in the absence of a listener. Like a real conversation, it involves a listener. So writing isn't writing unless it contemplates its listener, and attends to the listener's needs—in particular their need to understand at speed. It doesn't matter what you and your boss think of it: how good your writing is will be judged by the person at the receiving end. You can never be sure how much sense your writing makes for a reader you don't always get to meet, but it's your job never to stop trying. To make sense, that is. For just about anybody.

It's the writer's job, in other words, to stand in the reader's shoes, to want what the reader wants. You write for someone *else*. It isn't yourself you have to persuade. So it won't do much good to leave the slender particulars unsaid, the argument unmade, or the real truth unspoken. If a reader can't find it in your sentence, you haven't said it.

Don't ever forget: someone's listening; it's for their sake you're writing.

But don't worry *exactly* who they are. You can always be sure of this: everyone wants clarity; they want accomplished talking. So think of your reader—no matter who precisely they are and how many of them and how they differ—as an intelligent person who wants you to make perfect sense at a reasonable clip. Beyond that, they'd like a good time. If you can't do that, just get to the point.

You don't need to tailor each message, as though it were a suit, to fit its reader perfectly, for it never will. Your message is not a suit, and you'll never find enough ways to cut it to fit all your readers in their almost infinite variety. But if you write clearly, making the kind of perfect sense that just about anyone would understand; if you attend to the conversational rhythms and rich but familiar diction that most of us like to hear, you give yourself the best chance to reach your readers.

If you must tailor something, tailor your sentences. Cut them to the shape and size of the message you're trying to send; make them say nothing but what you mean to say.

How can anyone ever know, anyway, what each reader wants? And where would we find the time and 'resource' for that kind of market segmentation? Write instead what every reader wants. Work away at making sense for everyone. Write intelligently and intelligibly. That'll take most readers most of the way home.

Until you've worked out what you want to say—the particular story you want to tell of the facts you've got—don't worry who your readers are. Put your readers in parentheses until you've got your story straight. Clarity first, we say to clients, from bureaucrats to undergrads; politics second.

But if you imagine writing as a conversation, if you make yourself talk on paper (trimmer and tauter and more terrific than speech, but speech all the same), you'll always keep your reader in sight.

Writing is an act of empathy; it's not a practice of market segmentation. Really good writing is really good for everyone; it's readable by nearly anyone. That ought to be your aim, anyway: to exclude no one—neither the most expert nor the least knowledgeable.

6 Begin at the end

Look, it's not a state secret. If it were, you wouldn't be writing it.

So whatever your writing adds up to—write it down, right at the start. If not right at the start, then somewhere your reader can find it at speed.

A report, a thesis or a proposal is not a detective novel, so don't keep your readers in suspense. Tell them who did it, and tell them what's to be done about it—right there on page one. No one wants to read 136 pages to find out, if they're lucky, what you meant from the start (and may well have been trying not to say).

All the research on reader behaviour draws the same conclusion: draw your conclusion at the start. And yet one of the most common problems with the documents we see is their failure at or near the start, or sometimes anywhere, to tell the reader what the whole document concludes, proposes, recommends or offers for sale.

Remember; like you, your reader has better things to do. Let them know why you're troubling them, tell them what they'll find out if they read on and what good that may do them.

Good writers summarise, and readers love them for it and read on. Michael Pollan, for example, begins *In Defense of Food* like this:

> Eat food. Not too much. Mostly plants.

There is his book in miniature, his argument in outline. His beginning tells us where we will end; it sets the course (his as writer, ours as reader) for the country of the book. Explaining and justifying these three propositions will carry him and us to the close of his book.

Here are a few more good summaries.

> The transition to a low-carbon economy will bring challenges for competitiveness but also opportunities for growth.

> Timely warnings save lives. The community expects and depends on detailed and high quality information prior to, during, and after bushfires. The community is also entitled to receive timely and accurate bushfire warnings whenever possible, based on the intelligence available to the control agencies.

> Discontinuous change requires discontinuous thinking. If the new way of things is going to be different from the old, not just an improvement on it, then we shall need to look at everything in a new way.

> Men who drink alcohol have a reduced incidence of coronary heart disease (CHD), according to a study, published in the November 19 Online First issue of *Heart*.

The summaries that start stories in newspapers are called leads. Journalists take a lot of trouble to nail them. The idea is to tell the whole story, in outline, but excluding no material details, in the opening sentence or two. There should be names, numbers, quantities, times, places, causes, consequences. There'll be an invitation to read on: obviously a sentence can't contain a whole report or tell the full story; but there should be enough there to point to this one story in particular and to make me, if I have an interest, look deeper into the body of the document for more context, argument, justification, elaboration, colour, texture, light and shade. But I should find nothing in the full story not anticipated in the lead, and nothing that contradicts it. Here are a few good leads, the first from a novel, the others from newspapers.

> He was an old man who fished alone in a skiff in the Gulf Stream and he had gone eighty-four days now without taking a fish.
>
> The Black Hawk helicopter that crashed off Fiji in November, killing two soldiers, was a flight destined for disaster: that was the assessment yesterday of counsel assisting a military board of inquiry into the tragedy.
>
> Internet speeds will be forty times faster within five years, no matter who wins the next election.
>
> Three wars have broken out in a quiet Paddington street.
>
> For six years, an Amtrak engineer, Said Marcos, quietly awarded air-conditioning contracts to his mates, landing him $750,000, the corruption watchdog has found.
>
> The devil will be in the detail, philanthropy experts warn, despite widespread rapture over the Higher Education Endowment Fund (HEEF).

What's good for a newspaper is just as good for a report or a business letter. And since one thing most reports do is draw a conclusion and make some recommendations, that conclusion and those recommendations should be there in your lead sentence or two. (*The Little Red Writing Book* discusses the nature of a good lead, or thesis statement at p. 231, noting that 'a thesis is what you make of the evidence; it's your summary of what you've found. It should be clear and short and engaging—perhaps even intriguing. And it should open out into the exploration the rest of the document undertakes.') This summary doesn't do any of that.

> A number of external and internal environmental factors are driving the need for a well-planned, effectively coordinated IT strategy.

What factors? How many? How do they drive the need? What ends would the strategy meet?

Instead of this kind of thing,

> This strategic plan represents a statement of the vision for the information management future of the department.

write down, right there, what that vision is.

If you've reached a conclusion, if you have a thesis (reached by subjecting your hypothesis to rigorous analysis and testing), if you're making a recommendation, if all your looking and finding amounted to something—say what it is. Don't just say that your document does some looking, analysing, reviewing, considering, finding, concluding and recommending; summarise it.

We have more to say about the art of the summary—and we offer more examples of good leads—when we explore executive summaries in chapter 4.

7 Don't just do something—sit there

The better you plan your writing off the paper, the better it reads on.

Although good talking, supported by the character and gestures of the talker, can wander fruitfully about, good writing needs a straighter course. Listening while someone talks their way toward a conclusion can sometimes be enthralling, but that's the joy of finding yourself in the presence of a good storyteller, one of the foundations of entertainment, regardless of the medium through which it's delivered. Reading while a writer makes up his mind what he thinks he's telling you—that's agonising. And in business, doubly so. We're not looking to be entertained; rather, we're looking for answers, and if we don't get them, quickly and clearly, that can be awfully costly. Readers demand order, and the order must be that much more orderly than when you talk: writing and reading go slower and proceed more abstractly than conversation.

So finish your thinking before you start your writing. Arrive at your conclusion, and the structure of your case, before you start making it. Get yourself a plan.

We have more to say about this, the use of mindmapping in particular, in chapter 5; and chapter 6 of *The Little Red Writing Book* explores the thinking and planning part of the writing business at some length.

Your first draft needn't be—it almost certainly won't be—as tidy as you need to make the document in the end; there is some overlap between the end of the thinking and the start of the writing. But if you're still working out what you're trying to say, you're not writing yet—you're thinking (see the next item). The best writing gives a reader a feeling of profound order—you feel that the writer has worked out every heading, and every paragraph and every sentence within it before she laid them down so neatly.

A very good example of this orderliness every document should aspire to is the executive summary of *The Stern Review.*

The subheadings Stern uses summarise the summary and, indeed, the whole report. You could read it, as it were, at speed, simply by scanning the subheadings. Here are some of them.

- The benefits of strong, early action on climate change

outweigh the costs [This is the overall conclusion in the two-page summary of the whole summary]

- The scientific evidence points to increasing risks of serious, irreversible impacts from climate change associated with business-as-usual (BAU) paths for emissions
- Climate change threatens the basic elements of life for people around the world—access to water, food production, health, and use of land and the environment
- The damages from climate change will accelerate as the world gets warmer
- The impacts of climate change are not evenly distributed—the poorest countries and people will suffer earliest and most
- Emissions have been, and continue to be, driven by economic growth; yet stabilisation of greenhouse-gas concentrations in the atmosphere is feasible and consistent with continued growth
- Achieving these deep cuts in emissions will have a cost. The Review estimates the annual costs of stabilisation at 500–550 ppm CO_2e to be around 1% of GDP by 2050—a level that is significant but manageable
- The transition to a low-carbon economy will bring challenges for competitiveness but also opportunities for growth
- Reducing the expected adverse impacts of climate change is therefore both highly desirable and feasible
- Policy to reduce emissions should be based on three essential elements: carbon pricing, technology policy, and removal of barriers to behavioural change
- Building and sustaining collective action is now an urgent challenge
- There is still time to avoid the worst impacts of climate change if strong collective action starts now

There's no way Stern and his team could have achieved such order and clarity without a lot of planning, built up from a clear-headed deduction of the major conclusions they drew from their long, slow reading of the science and their equally painstaking modelling of the economics of climate change.

Stern's reading of the science and his econometrics have been called into some question; such criticism is, of course, the way knowledge develops. But the thinking—about an enormously emotive and disputed and alarming set of issues—and its articulation in circumspect, clear and simple prose stand as models for any functional writer.

And if it can be done for the toughest issue of our times, it can probably be done on whatever project it is you have in front of you.

We have more to say on executive summaries in chapter 4; and more to say about the art of the summary in chapter 5.

8 No—we're *not* there yet

Most writers pull up short—especially busy business writers. As consultants, we read a lot of emails, advices, reports and allegedly finished papers that are replete with errors of fact and sense, syntax and spelling and style—things that escape a writer's notice in an early draft, but shouldn't when she reads it again and again and, yes, again.

In a writing class one day, one man, an experienced writer, cleared his throat before he read a piece he'd just written: 'Forgive this', he said; 'it's five drafts short of finished.' Until you start wrecking it, writing gets better the more attention you pay it.

There's so much to do when you write—having the thought; having the next one; getting them straight; forgetting every silly thing everyone ever told you about commas and conjunctions at the start of the sentence; thinking too much about who your readers are and why they probably hate you—no one can get it all done at a sitting. Writing is recursive, by nature; it takes several goes—it's *meant* to take several goes—to get it down the clear-headed way it spoke itself to you in your head before you opened the file.

And then at work there are all those other pressures and anxieties, among them getting the report finished before it's due to be tabled, not to mention keeping your job. There are distractions; there is the fact that you simply don't really know enough about this topic. There's the anxiety, among academics (especially postgraduate students), that you've probably misunderstood the other authorities, and probably haven't discovered most of them anyway. In business, there's the risk that you'll subject your business to some kind of liability or commitment; in government, there's the fear you're committing some kind of policy gaffe or political atrocity.

It's going to take several goes. And so it should: it's going to last.

So don't mistake your first draft for your last.

Think of writing as a project, and manage it. There are all the stages of research and preparation; there's the writing; and there's all the rewriting, out of which the piece of writing you sat to write will, with luck and grace, but more likely as a result of the requisite hard work, emerge. You're going to need time, so make it. You're going to need three or four drafts at least, so get the first started earlier than you'd thought, and build in time at the end for as many rewrites as you think you'll need, and more. If you haven't left enough time—beg some, make some, borrow some, steal some. Or else reconcile yourself to an unfinished document and everything it will say about you and how much less it will say to your reader than it might.

Would you launch a new product onto the market before it was ready? Would you re-brand your organisation without exhaustive research, development and market testing? So why would you release a piece of writing—which will quite likely be on the record in perpetuity—half-baked?

An unedited document is an unfinished house. It will not stand; it will not keep the weather out or the contents in. Just when you think you're finished editing, do it one more time.

9 The short words are best

English, being English, and not, for instance, French or German, goes best when the words are short; the sentences, on the other hand, can be as long as they like. It should surprise no one that we've made a fetish of short sentences in an era when we know much less than we once did about sentences, and how to make them sound good, and long. Truth is, good sentences come long and short, and good paragraphs love them all. A good sentence is about as long as it needs to be: the question is not how long, but how good. And sentences work best when they're made of short, familiar words strung together in interesting ways.

While writers in business and science, government and the professions have been out there for centuries now favouring long words and convoluted phrasing, as though professionalism demanded some sort of elevation of the tongue, great writers—poets, playwrights, novelists, essayists and journalists—have kept writing beautiful prose remarkably close, in diction and structure, to speech—speech tidied and trimmed, enlivened by an exquisite unfamiliar word, it's true, here and there, but not frocked up.

> What a piece of work is a man, how noble in reason, how infinite in faculties, in form and moving how express and admirable, in action how like an angel.

> All good things come by grace and grace comes by art and art does not come easy.

> Read a few pages of Emily Dickinson and then go and see Von Trier's film *Dogville*. In Dickinson's poetry the presence of the eternal is attendant in every pause. The film, by contrast, remorselessly shows what happens when any trace of the eternal is erased from daily life.

> We must return to our bodies; life reclaims us. We must look, together, at the world that surrounds us. We must go farther, until we encounter the unknown.

Of course, it's not as straightforward as that; some fine creative writing is ornate and Byzantine. One school of thought about literature, identifiable with George Orwell, will tell you that the purpose of one's writing is to get out of the way; prose, Orwell thought, should be a window—a transparent revelation of one's meaning. By contrast, Samuel Beckett once said that the purpose of his writing was to draw a veil across his meaning. This is the other school, then: writing as a beautiful puzzle. There is a kind of literature, of which William Faulkner would be another example, where the writing, more than the meaning, is the point. You're meant to notice and be astonished by the sentences, in the same way you're arrested, now and then, by the lay of the land, or by a woman or a man or by the face of a child—and then you're meant, as in life, to stand and wonder, for as long as it takes, at what the text, in its body, has to say to you.

But even such writing aims to veil and baffle *beautifully*—which is to say that the feint, the subtending of meaning, is deliberately, graciously and artistically performed, and is pleasing in itself. It's a mask. But this is a place we don't want to go in business; let's put away the masks; it's hard to dissemble and mislead with grace or virtue when the reader has no interest in being beguiled.

'Words, like nature', as Tennyson said, may 'half reveal and half conceal the soul within', but this is business, so let's concentrate on the *revealing* part, and see if we can get a little closer than halfway to what we mean to say.

Here's how the principle of beautiful simplicity, shapely strings of short words, can work at work.

> Many doctors now offer Medicare electronic claiming. It's a fast, secure system that allows you to make your Medicare claim at the doctor's when you pay your account.

> From its origins in 1914 as a Western Australian farmers' cooperative, Wesfarmers has grown into one of Australia's largest listed companies and

employers. Its business operations cover supermarkets, department stores, home improvement and office supplies; coal mining; energy; insurance; chemicals and fertilisers; and industrial and safety products.

> Regardless of the particular data quality issue, the department needs to resolve who is responsible for the integrity of its data. This is both a persistent and strategic issue. Currently, much depends on the soundness of the original data entry by any of several thousand staff. There is no substantial edit-checking at data entry to ensure the quality of the information entered.

The habit, entrenched in business prose, of favouring the long and indirect over the short and plain is known as 'false elegance'. It arises, like most bad habits, from fear. In this case, fear that you won't sound businesslike, smart and expensive unless your language is impenetrable. Whole novels have been written parodying this sad and stubborn addiction, but of course it persists. George Orwell's 'Politics and the English Language' targets it. Don Watson has written three books critiquing the deathly, voiceless and dehumanising prose of managerialism, the modern incarnation of this habit. Mark makes his case against it in *The Little Red Writing Book*, relying, among others, on Walter Murdoch, who argued: beware the man who favours long words—either he doesn't know what he's talking about or he doesn't want you to know.

Here are two instances of the kind of thing Murdoch had in his sights.

> The ongoing emergence of a strategy of scaled innovation, together with the sourcing and development of human capital is designed to maximise the Group's return on investment going forward.

> We aim to facilitate a paradigm shift in the way we impact the market at all levels by engaging with stakeholders in an ongoing dialogue that acknowledges our commitment to accountability.

Both of them grandiose, conforming, nonsense.

Because English is at its leanest and loveliest when short words are deftly joined to compose shapely phrases and clauses; because it's closer to how we make sense of things with the words in our mouths; and because short words are more efficient than long ones, be suspicious of words of more than two syllables. Ration them; use them with care.

Short is smart: until you can put a thing simply, you probably haven't thought it through. We use long words, wrote Walter Murdoch, 'when we want to hide our thought or the fact that we have not thought at all'.

Short is also rhythmic: 'We have nothing to fear but fear itself' (said Franklin D Roosevelt); 'The art of losing isn't hard to master' (wrote Elizabeth Bishop); 'Do not go gentle into that good night' (wrote Dylan Thomas); 'We work in the dark, we do what we can, we give what we have; our doubt is our passion, our passion is our task—and the rest is the madness of art' (wrote Henry James); 'There is one timeless way of building. It is thousands of years old, and the same today as it has always been' (wrote Christopher Alexander); 'You can't miss the alpine flowers at Thredbo; they grow higher than the trees' (said the advertisement Jack Vaughan wrote); 'We work with other government agencies to coordinate Australia's pursuit of its global, regional and bilateral interests' (wrote the elegant bureaucrat).

But writing in short words will find you out: there's nowhere to hide when the language is transparent and straight—no room for obfuscation, boast and evasion.

What would this next piece mean, for instance, dressed not in an ill-fitting tuxedo, but in jeans and a tee-shirt; what would this actually say, if it spoke plainly? What, exactly, does this department do, and what is it for, when you strip it of rhetoric?

> The Department of Education, Employment and Workplace Relations (DEEWR) is a dynamic, innovative and customer-focused organisation that contributes to strong employment growth, increased workforce participation and the improved productive performance of enterprises in Australia.

Well, a reader might comment, you say you're dynamic and innovative and customer-focused, but how would I know, and why would I care, and what's in it for me? And what, exactly, is the nature of the contribution you make to no less than the 'improved productive performance' of the nation?

You get to find out in the next paragraph or two, but what then, was the opening paragraph for? Spin? Why would we think anyone would be interested in, and fooled by, reading that? Ah, this looks more promising:

> We use current and emerging technologies to improve our customer service and to help connect people to jobs and promote the transition from welfare to work.
>
> The Department of Education, Employment and Workplace Relations provides access to online services and information, guiding you to employment information, government assistance, jobs, careers, training, working conditions and Indigenous Employment Centres.

But why talk about 'current and emerging technologies' before telling us what the department uses them for—which is the point? Not more spin, surely? And where, in all this, is the 'education' in the department's name?

This doesn't sound like an arm of the public sector, delivering policy research and advice to government and administering projects; it sounds like a library or an employment agency. What is happening to language here? It's all show, and no go. Like so much writing in the public domain.

There is an aesthetic principle that works in most fields, writing included, the principle of elegance: less is more. What this means in writing is that you use only as many words as you need to say exactly what you mean. There's scope, as *The Little Red Writing Book* shows, for quite wide variation in personal styles; but good writing feels tight, trim. As though there is no fat upon it.

Divorce may be the end of a marriage, but it is not the end of the family.

To buy an insurance policy, select from the list below or call us on 123456.

Until 30 June, the government is virtually giving money away. Regrettably, most people won't bother to take it. From 10 May till 30 June 2004 you can make a one-off undeducted contribution of up to $1 million into your super fund. What benefits will you enjoy if you act before 30 June? Say you're around 40 and you're setting up your future (as everyone should be now). You'll only pay 15 percent tax on your increased super investment income, rather than the marginal tax rate, which could be as high as 46.5 percent … There's a lot to consider, so you may want to seek some advice.

Why not save yourself a trip to the motor registry and renew your rego online? It's the fast and easy option. Plus you can access six months short-term rego, which is only available online or over the phone.

This next piece is body copy from a magazine advertisement for a car, so, yeah, they had a little more room to move than you probably have where you sit. But don't be too quick to dismiss it. You may not feel able to stretch a sentence quite so long or ease its diction quite so far back in your line of work, but everyone could learn a lot from this piece about the punch of verbs and the charm of the vernacular. And if you're in marketing, here's a masterclass.

It doesn't last forever (in fact it goes all too quickly) but there is a time when you have to carry lots of things and pick up and drop off lots of people and be in five places at once and be there on time in case they're standing around waiting in the street never thinking the traffic's as bad as it looks from where you sit, which is luckily high and cozy, and you start to think as you manage to squeak through one set of green lights then the next that what with Trajet's pulling power and all it's got going for it that this is one household appliance that's actually almost fun. Because you have to fit it all in: Trajet.

10 Where have all the people gone?

Most business writing works hard to leave the people out. It avoids, where it can, naming anyone (person or even department) as the agent of any action; it abjures personal pronouns (first (*I*) and even second (*you*)). It trades, where it can, in concepts and abstractions.

> It was found, as a result of investigations conducted over a period of time, that there was considerable scope for review with respect to the manner in which alignment of resources with stated outcomes and objectives was pursued.

> The success of the project will be largely dependent upon the ability of XYZ resources to be able to attend workshops ... preparation of user acceptance test plans and complete acceptance testing ...

> The implementation of the solution at DEFT Learnings will accommodate the shared services accounts payable requirements. It provides a complete solution enabling management of the payment process and bank account funding a reconciliation.

> A strong corporate governance regime imposes an alignment of authority, responsibility and accountability within an entity.

> It was a conclusion of a recent study that a positive correlation exists between reduced incidence of coronary heart disease and the consumption of moderate to high levels of alcohol.

> Safe and rational prescribing relies on complete and accurate records of current medications being kept.

Objectivity is the game here—a worthy, if illusory, ideal. Academics, scientists, lawyers, business people, bureaucrats, project managers, account managers and fire chiefs aren't writing memoirs, of course. They should spare us their inner lives. But they are telling us the story of the facts. They are people, whatever else they happen to be; their organisations, too, are made up of people. People doing things, in fact. The experiments and programs and products of these people, alone and in collaboration, involve human agency and impacts, and that should be implicit, even explicit, in the writing. Again—this is not memoir; nor is it a love song. So the banker and the scholar, the bureaucrat and the doctor ought to write objectively, yes; but they'd do better to write engagingly and concretely, too, in a mode that makes some kind of actual sense and lets a reader envisage what they are being told.

Leaving people out kills off your sentences; you can only do it using tired and soporific syntactical tricks like an excess of the passive voice, nominalisation, the abstraction of subject and object, the emasculation of verbs, the use of noun clusters (for more on all these, by the way, see *The Little Red Writing Book*). Readers understand best the story a sentence tells when they can discern with ease *who is doing what*. When they can find a *verb* and work out *who*'s performing it and upon *what or whom*. These are, of course, the three principal roles on offer in that magical structure of meaning, the sentence: subject, verb and object. You can find the *who does what* with ease in this paragraph. It is plain and concrete enough, though its subject matter is technical: prescription and disease. Its sentences are plain, and there are some people ('children') and things ('throat,' 'nose', 'ear' and 'membrane') in here. The verbs, admittedly, are not especially strong ('is', 'are', 'predict', 'have'), but the sentences seem to describe the actual world.

> The cause of URTI (upper respiratory tract infection) is usually viral … Secretions for throat and nose are common in uncomplicated URTI. They do not predict bacterial infection or benefit from antibiotic treatment. Many children with viral URTI have accompanying mild inflammation of the middle ear, with visible redness and dulling of the tympanic membrane.

So use some verbs and put some people (yourself included) back in your sentences (we'll italicise the verbs).

> The Tax Office *is* the Government's principal revenue collection agency, and *is* part of the Treasurer's portfolio. We *manage* and *shape* tax, excise and superannuation systems that *fund* services for Australians.

> We *recruit* the brightest lawyers we *can find*; we *value* the freshness of their ideas, and the originality of their thinking; we *set* them *to work* with experienced partners, and we *believe* that the combination of youth and experience, imagination and wisdom *helps* our clients *find* the most creative and lasting solutions to their business challenges.

The second example lives and breathes and talks because it is so rich with everyday verbs. And because it deploys so many words of action it is compelled to cast a whole bunch of real-life characters ('we', 'lawyers', 'partners', 'clients') as well as some tangible abstractions ('freshness of their ideas', 'originality of their thinking', 'youth and experience, imagination and wisdom', 'creative and lasting solutions', 'business challenges') to perform and receive those actions.

Ideology and politics are at work, of course, as well as custom, in leaving people (including the speaker) out of sentences in functional writing. It helps business and science and government extend their claims over us, over all life, if they write people out. Impersonality and abstraction impute importance and necessity to decisions and actions and conclusions. They allow truths to be hidden. They provide cover for careless, unfinished thinking. But, to be fair, most people write this way from habit, not intent; or they write this way because someone has told them it's what the profession or the firm or the academic world requires—the only conceivable way, apparently, to pull off the trick of objectivity.

'Only he who takes what he writes directly out of his own head is worth reading' wrote Schopenhauer, advocating the primary virtues of voice and self-reliance in writing, and thinking of the limits of scholarly writing and the merits, by contrast, of essays (like those of Montaigne and Darwin, perhaps), not to mention literature, that wisdom vehicle. Meanwhile, ignoring him and all that stuff, many universities specifically (and misguidedly) instruct students these days to write impersonally—to favour the passive voice and never to use the first-person personal pronoun (more on this below).

If impersonality is a learned behaviour, unlearn it; learn critical thought and its expression instead. What is wanted is personal writing that's dispassionate and detached. The impersonal corrupts language, distorts messages and muddles thinking (yours and your reader's). It makes life harder than it should be for the very people you're trying to engage; it generates more noise than light.

11 Assertiveness 101

Write assertively—not, as is more common, defensively, passive-aggressively, stuffily or vaguely.

Clarity, admittedly, is hard work. It's difficult to think your way to the end of a thought and set it down plainly. There are techniques of composition, tricks of rhetoric and rules of grammar that too many writers know too little about. But difficulty is only part of the reason so much functional writing is so murky—so meek or oblique, bland or evasive or awkward.

Courage—or the lack of it—is another reason. Bad writing is not only tolerated, it is expected and rewarded, and it takes courage to resist. One often has to argue hard for clarity; one has to make a special pleading for transparency and sense. For obfuscation is conventional. Pomp and obscurity are business, government and academic addictions—excused constantly, as though clarity were either beyond or beneath us. 'Oh, but the journals expect longwinded writing', they tell us; 'oh, but my boss is very old school and likes this kind of thing'; 'but if I write it simply, it'll only get changed in middle management'.

Even if these complaints are true, your reader loses and your writing fails if you give in to them. Not to mention the language and yourself.

And, in truth, enough good writing cuts through—it gets published, it overcomes the resistance of middle management, it is awarded a higher degree, it gets tabled and read, it wins annual report and plain English prizes—to know that clarity has a market. You just have to find a way. And that takes courage.

Good writers write like they mean it—in whatever field they find themselves in. They write as though they know we're listening. They speak. They use words as soft weapons for telling the truth and doing some good, including to themselves. They tell whatever it is they have to tell, as close as possible to how it really is; they show you what it looks like and tell you why it matters in the real world. Plainly, humanely, carefully, sparely.

A thesis or a report is not poetry, but it *is* a story: the story of what you did, or what you think, or what you propose, of what you found when you went looking and what conclusions you drew; the tale of how things really go, or how you think they should.

So, step up. Shrug off the fear of what you think others might think. Overcome your fear of simplicity, and your attachment to the security of convolution. Say it in words that taste right in your mouth and sound good in your ear. Assert yourself.

12 Coin clichés—don't parrot them

Clichés come like this: *going forward*, *push the envelope*, *sea change*, *tree change*, *scalable*, *benchmark* (both the noun and the verb), *align*, *drivers*, *green shoots*, *support*, *iterative* and *leverage*.

And like this: *further to*, *in relation to*, *on a regular basis*, *should you have any further questions in this regard please do not hesitate to contact myself*, *prior to that*, *this role has responsibility for*, *it is incumbent upon us*, *deliverables*, *outcomes*, *value-adding*, *drivers of change*, *taking ownership* and *task-oriented*.

Here are some more: *innovation*, *emerging*, *embedded*, *sustainability*, *synergy* and *organic*. Start clustering them, in the manner of *organic innovation*, or perhaps *embedded sustainability*, or, for goodness sake, *embedded innovation and organic sustainability*, and what's left of your credibility will most likely be in tatters. With discriminating readers, that is—people who still want language to actually mean something. Your colleagues won't appear to notice, and your bosses may reward you: such atrocities are commonplace; they are almost *de rigueur*.

But this is tired and emotionless language, and it's not your own. It belongs to someone else. It's bankrupt and foolish. It lacks life; it's unclear; it fills space with sound but not with sense. The best that can be said for it is that it's convenient: using it saves you the trouble of thinking; it spares you from saying something real, to which you or your organisation might be held accountable. It's lazy and empty, and it sounds that way to your readers. It's also infuriating.

Lately the editors of newspapers and magazines, even the headline writers for the television news, seem to have convinced themselves that the only way to introduce a story is with a pun or a word play, often rather obvious. Once in a while, this practice can have power. But the habit itself has become a cliché, and many of the turns of phrase are pretty weak. Spare us, please, the airline company that has 'struck turbulence', the mining company that's 'sunk deeper into a hole', the rain that 'has dampened the enthusiasm of festival goers' or the investors who have 'hung up on the telecommunications giant'.

If you want clichés, coin them. Don't parrot; speak. If you don't want the trouble of turning out fresh tropes, just write plainly what you mean.

13 A bonus tip—write sentences, not dot points

We live in the era of the dot point. In some places these days, people don't write any more; they PowerPoint.

Now, dot points, used sparingly, are a powerful rhetorical device.

India has certain advantages (over China, for instance) that will help it survive the rapid economic growth it has begun:

- its open society
- its robust democracy
- its culture of pluralism and tolerance
- its gift for language.

Plain English encourages writers to

- write readable sentences
- get to their point fast
- choose a layout that reveals the shape of their thinking.

Use dot points to articulate the structure and emphasise the sense of a sentence—to take its key points and lay them out in a neat stack before a reader. Use them as slides, and talk them into some semblance of meaning.

But don't let dot points stand in for sentences. For sentences are the smartest system the language knows for making meaning fast. If you haven't written a sentence—a sound, orthodox piece of syntax—you probably haven't worked out what you mean. Dot points, used in place of sentences, may save you some time, but they make a reader work too hard.

More on this in chapter 5.

CHAPTER 3

SEVEN HEAVENLY VIRTUES

To put all this another way: there are seven deadly sins of business writing and seven heavenly virtues.

Foreswear the former, observe the latter, and write your way—and your readers' way—out of business writing hell.

Beware all rubrics, of course, including the one that follows. They always oversimplify; this one oversimplifies a tremendously complicated business—writing on time and on budget in the real world. All the same, this list arises from two decades of deep immersion in and quiet late-night reflection upon the best and worst habits of functional writers. And it offers a business writer a powerful tool for critically appraising and improving their own work. See the virtues as stretch goals; view the vices—many of which may look at first a lot like how you learned to write at work and how you thought you had to—as underperformance. Forgive these moral-sounding imperatives. Sometimes it's only the fear of god or the promise of paradise that helps us change our ways.

The seven deadly sins	The seven heavenly virtues
Profligacy	Economy
Neglect	Care
Selfishness	Empathy
Pomp	Cool
Obscurity	Clarity
Clunk	Flow
Haste	Finish

Good business writing is—to put this adjectivally—economical, careful, empathetic, cool (as in informal and dignified), clear, fluent and finished. Bad writing is profligate, neglectful, selfish, pompous (stilted, bossy, stiff, false), obscure, clunky (incoherent and hard to follow) and hasty (two or three drafts short of done).

From what we've said about the twelve big ideas in the last chapter, you'll have a fair notion of what each of these adjectives means at your keyboard. But let's explain them a little and offer some examples.

1 Economical/profligate

Economical writing says a lot with a little; it's trim, thrifty and intelligently simple. It avoids false elegance; it favours the short word over the long, everyday diction over formal expressions. It will sound like tidied talking.

The currency we trade in is sentences, and the best ones, as we've noted, string together short, familiar words in pleasing, revealing and interesting ways. To write in short, familiar words is not to dumb down; it's to wise up. Take the trouble to make something difficult plain, and your reader will thank you—you'll have made them feel more intelligent. They'll see you as someone who knows their subject well enough to put it simply enough to share.

Many organisations work hard to write in plain English because it makes good business sense; saying a lot with a little is bound to please your customers more than saying a little with a lot. Plain English organisations understand that by communicating well with their stakeholders, they build stronger relationships. Of course, plain English doesn't mean leaving the hard stuff out—the technical details, the complex arguments, the policy contexts. Some documents have to cover ideas and instruments, products and policies that are unfamiliar to the reader and hard to fathom. These organisations know that using plain English, in particular short everyday words put together in sentences shaped the way we shape them in speech, is the surest strategy for making sense for their readers of complex material.

Profligate writing says a little with a lot; it's flabby, wasteful of syllables and unnecessarily complicated. It makes a virtue of its addiction to false elegance; it favours the long word over the short, technical diction over perfectly serviceable, transparently meaningful everyday words and phrases. It will sound like unkempt, tin-eared discourse.

Here are some examples of economical business writing.

> Many critics believe that the main cause of the global financial crisis is that financial institutions acted imprudently because of inadequate controls and adverse management compensation systems. In this talk we will argue—to the contrary—that the crisis resulted from lack of awareness of the consequences of mixing optimal risk management practices with inadequate regulation that created enormous capital market imperfections. We also suggest what an optimal regulatory system might look like in the future.

> We deliver what we promise. We'll get your package where you want it when you want it in the condition it was in when you gave it to us. Or your money back.

> RT is one of the world's leading mining companies. We find, mine and process the earth's mineral resources—metals essential for making

thousands of everyday products that meet society's needs and improve living standards.

This study looks at the complexities facing airline managements, and in particular at (1) the problems facing a new airline seeking to establish itself in a network industry, especially when entering city-pair markets already served by others, and (2) the responses of incumbents to such entry.

And profligacy goes like this.

The estimation of loss reserves for incurred but not reported (IBNR) claims presents an important task for insurance companies to predict their liabilities. Conventional methods, such as ladder or separation methods based on aggregated or grouped claims in the form of 'run-off triangle', have been illustrated to have some drawbacks. Recently, individual claim loss models have been introduced to overcome the shortcomings of aggregated claim loss models, but they have limitations too.

The growth rates of workplace injury and illness rates exhibit a negative (time varying) mean and a pro-cyclical response to variations in economic activity, as they decline in recessions before rebounding (and overshooting) during economic recoveries. Using a structural time series model, it is shown that this business cycle behavior is driven by job flows. In recessions, the acceleration of job destruction increases the growth rate of workplace injury and illness incidence rate (which is indicative of moral hazard), while the slowdown in job creation depresses this growth rate by reducing the proportion of workers of short job tenure.

An exciting opportunity has arisen to join a committed and highly motivated group with a view to progressing a highly leveraged change agenda in a prestigious cutting edge organisation. Tertiary qualified with postgraduate experience and professional development, you will be a team player with the capability to exhibit dynamic leadership qualities and inspirational values focussed thought leadership.

A grass fire is burning 3 kilometres east of Kilmore, near Saunders Road (VicRoads Map reference 417 C4). It is burning in a southeasterly

> direction. This fire is not currently posing a threat to communities, however the communities of Kilmore East, Wandong and Clonbinane need to be aware of this fire. This fire has now jumped the Hume Highway and significant spotting has occurred. The fire is impacting on the outskirts of the Wandong township.

This (last) example has some upside: it uses some real-world nouns/noun phrases ('grass fire', 'spotting', 'communities', 'township') and verbs ('is burning', 'jumped'). And its sentences are short. But you're still left feeling the paragraph could do with a good burn. The wastefulness comes in part from truncation of sentences, which forces the writer to repeat 'this fire/the fire' and 'is burning'. Then there are 'in a southeasterly direction', 'is impacting on' and 'not currently posing a threat'—unkempt and hackneyed bureaucratic usages—and that usual suspect 'significant', which we get so used to hearing we stop believing.

Hear how awkwardly and obliquely this next sentence tries (or perhaps doesn't try hard enough) to tell us that two reports, the year before, made clear how critical it is for the department to know beyond doubt whom it's dealing with.

> The need to clearly establish identity and to ensure a consistent identity is sustained was highlighted during 2005, when two inquiry reports were released that made recommendations in relation to how the department manages the identity of its clients.

Surely it would surprise these 'clients', referred to in the same report as 'refugee and humanitarian clients', to know that they are 'clients'. Clients have a choice in the matter, and they tend to pay for the service they choose to receive. Refugees and immigrants, both legal and illegal, have not, on the whole, approached the department for a service; and if they have, they have little choice in the matter.

By the way, the department's strategic plan we quote from goes on to note coyly that the two inquiries 'found limitations in the department's ability to accurately identify its clients and to match or correlate variations in client records'. *Limitations in the department's ability*!

Australia's prime minister Kevin Rudd is said to be fond of backing up the truck and dumping facts, figures, details and acronyms into his speeches as his own special personal touch. He has also proven to be a serial offender in the matter of redundancy, as evidenced by this effort in a speech delivered in November 2008: 'By immediate, I mean immediate. Immediate means now. It's ready to go now.' Yes, prime minister.

2 Careful/neglectful

When you write with care, your sentences are sound (stylistically, grammatically, logically), unambiguous and smooth. We'd add that they took care about the needs of the reader, too, if that weren't the next virtue in this litany. We have in mind here the *care* you take with *what* you say (is this just what I mean to say?) and *how* you say it (are my sentences well crafted?).

By contrast, neglectful writing is carelessly made: your sentences are awkwardly worded; your syntax dodgy and your punctuation awry; your logic faulty or hard to fathom; your meaning ambiguous or uncertain.

Here's care at play.

> The framework clearly specifies the roles and responsibilities of each level of government; it improves reporting on performance; and it models a more collaborative working approach.

> At CR we take a considered approach to the way we conduct business. Wherever and however we can, we promote social and environmental change for the better.

> Chances are you have a good idea of where you want to go in life. At Google, we've designed a culture that helps you get there. From our flexible, project-based approach to corporate structure to our innovative

perks and benefits, we do everything we can to make sure our employees not only have great jobs, but great lives.

And here are some instances of neglect.

> This strategic plan articulates the business need for identity management, the internal and external operating environment, the business impacts and potential benefits for the Australian Government and society as well as the business ownership governance arrangements and key elements of the identity management strategy.

The writers of that sentence neglected their syntax; the sentence falls apart. (Some deft dots—laying out each separate item the plan is alleged to 'articulate'—would have helped here.) As it stands, it's almost impossible to follow.

> The PDRs revealed that the cost of building houses on the Tiwi Islands and Groote Eylandt was significantly higher than had been anticipated by the Australian Government. There were several contributing factors: First, the houses were being built in high cost locations ...

The high cost of building in those locations appears to have been overlooked in initial budget calculations. Telling us that the cost was significantly higher than anticipated because they were in high-cost locations is like a dog chasing its tail.

Note also how leaving the hyphen out of 'high-cost locations' creates some confusion at first about whether the costs or the locations were 'high'. A small piece of carelessness that doesn't help a reader much.

And who can really be sure what this means?

> Our aspiration is that our growth will strengthen our leading shares across chosen segments and products.

No doubt the company took some time to come up with that formulation; they probably paid a consultant a good fee to help them. But the care they all forgot to take was to say something unambiguous and specific to them as an organisation (which segments, what products, what is a 'leading share'?) Notice, too, how long 'our aspiration is that our growth will strengthen our leading shares' takes to say something that might more exactly and clearly be expressed as 'we aspire to increase our share'.

See if you can follow this.

> The capital works funding contributed by the Commonwealth was provided to the Northern Territory Government which would be the purchaser of program management and construction services for the program and the day to day program administrator.

As it stands, it seems like the Northern Territory Government is looking to purchase a program administrator. What they really mean is probably something like this: 'The Commonwealth provided capital works funding to help the Northern Territory Government secure program management and construction services for the program; under the agreement, the Northern Territory Government operates as the day-to-day administrator of the program.'

And finally some hip corporate obscurantism.

> We need out performance at every level—financial out performance, out performing in customer service and in our work ethic.

'Outperform' is a verb that makes sense when used transitively ('we want to outperform our competitors'); as a noun, *out performance* is awkward and unclear. (Another case of managerialism contorting language to express dodgy ideas?) And why *out performing* the third time the mongrel noun is used? Apart from the carelessness with diction, the structure of the sentence is shaky—in part because *financial*, *customer service* and *work ethic* aren't 'levels': two are areas of operation; the third is an attitude, a state of mind, or an aspect of culture. If all this really had to be said, maybe it would have worked better like this: 'We aim to outperform [stakeholder expectations] in our work ethic, and in every operating area—financial, customer service, marketing, backroom support.'

Richard Ford, that fine American writer, has spent his life struggling with dyslexia, which forces him to write very slowly; but it turns out his affliction is his gift. He is forced to weigh every word and parse every phrase, to make sure it makes the sense he had in mind, in exactly the way he had in mind, before the writing got in the way. And as a result, his prose is among the clearest and most admired of our age.

The moral? Take that kind of care, even though you'll think you don't have to. And if you're not dyslexic, take extra care. Barbara Blackman, a blind poet, once, in irritation and affliction, accused her sighted dinner party colleagues of being disabled by sight. (We couldn't find the CD player upstairs in her house or the place in the kitchen cabinet where the cleaned plates went without turning on the lights; we were disabled by our sightedness, in other words—by what we were able to do and she was not. She'd learned to pay closer attention and to feel her way more mindfully to her target.) Which is to say, your ability to string a few words together without difficulty may blind you to the many ways of stringing them together better.

Slow down. Do it again. As Samuel Beckett famously advised: 'Fail again. Fail better.'

3 Empathetic/selfish

Empathetic business writing remembers its reader and converses with them. It shapes sentences, and peoples them with words, calculated to deliver an unambiguous message with reasonable grace and speed to an intelligent reader in a hurry—not merely for the expert, the blow-in or the subject-matter virgin you think you're writing for. If your audience includes readers with varying levels of expertise, familiarity, engagement, attitude and literacy (in general or in the subject), empathy means you write to include all of them—or more precisely, to exclude none. And good, empathetic writers presume that their audience is always mixed and always in want of quick returns on their investment of time. It's a smart play; it'll incline you toward real words and sound sentences. Empathetic writing can go something like this.

> Women, during pregnancy, need around three times as much iron as they normally do. By far the best natural sources of dietary iron are lean beef, lamb, liver and kidneys. Because iron in these foods closely resembles the iron in our bodies, it's far more easily absorbed. Best of all, it's a way of taking iron that you can actually enjoy.

> With no change to the way we drive cars, burn coal, use power, raze forests and keep livestock, the population of the globe will emit about 58 gigatonnes—58 billion tonnes—of carbon dioxide each year by 2020.

> Tax expenditures have no generally agreed definition. In practice, what constitutes a tax expenditure can change over time and between jurisdictions.

> In 2006–07, tax expenditures provided over $41 billion of relief to taxpayers from Commonwealth taxes and charges. Delivered mostly as tax exemptions, reduced rates of tax and tax rebates, total assistance through tax expenditures is similar in size to assistance delivered through the Commonwealth's largest spending (or outlay) programs.

Selfish business writing forgets its reader; it converses with no one. It deposits on screen or paper some sentence-like aggregations of words, without much attention to how they might sound, and whether they might mean much to a flesh-and-blood human being impatient for meaning. Selfish writing is solipsistic, inhumane and frequently ridiculous. Written for nobody, it rarely means anything (which is sometimes its purpose, but should never be yours).

As an editorial in *The Australian* in October 2008 put it, 'Too many official documents and speeches these days are mired in ugly, obscurantist prose that defies interpretation. Lazy metaphors, jargon and acronyms have invaded the lexicon of public debate. Vagueness and pretension bury the meaning, leading to the suspicion that, in truth, the author simply doesn't know what he or she is talking about.'

By way of an optimistic response, consider this extract from a eulogy to a recently departed copy editor published in the *New York Times* in September 2008: 'Helene had no literary theories—she had literary values. She valued clarity and transparency. She had nothing against style, if it didn't distract from the material. Her blue pencil struck at redundancy, at confusion, at authorial vanity, at the wrong and the false word, at the unearned conclusion. She loved good writing, therefore she loved the reader: good writing did not cause the reader to stumble over meaning.'

Here's a fairly solipsistic explanation of why a national park is a national park, which almost certainly did a lot more for the writer than it does for readers.

> As noted in Section 2.6, the EPBC Act requires this Management Plan to assign the Park to an IUCN category. The EPBC Regulations prescribe the management principles for each IUCN category. The category to which the Park is assigned is guided by the purposes for which the Park was declared (see Section 2.4, Legislative context). The purposes for which Uluru–Kata Tjuta National Park was declared are consistent with the characteristics for IUCN protected area category II 'national park'.

Here, the writer might take a lead from the sales department. It's not about you; it's about your customers or, in the case of something you're writing, your readers, who may well be your customers in any case. They don't much care about your problems, or how clever you've been in compiling whatever it is that you've gone to the trouble of writing for them. They're reading for a purpose, which in some way is, ultimately, to solve a problem of some kind—such as, why you're writing to them; or to understand how you're going to help them, or why you can't; or to evaluate your organisation's performance over the previous financial year; or to appreciate why you don't want the parkland down the road to be turned into a golf course. It's about the old features and benefits thing, too. You've cross-referenced your narrative to layered spreadsheets? Good for you. But has that made your message any easier for your reader to fathom? If not, you've wasted your time, and theirs.

4 Cool/pompous

We're talking tone here—the attitude your writing gives off. The tone you strike is no accident; it's the way you sound because of the words and expressions you choose. And we choose words and adopt poses—relaxed and dignified or stiff and defensive—according to our level of ease and mastery. The masterful writer (in command of subject, syntax, self and style) is more likely to be cool (and consequently impressive, engaging and persuasive).

Cool writing is informal but respectful; relaxed but aware; detached but personable; simple but discerning; confident but humble; gracious but astute. Something like this.

> Success depends on clarity. About who you are and where you want to go and how you're going to get there in one piece. It's hard to stay that clear when the world grows smaller and spins faster each day, when technology and regulation grow more complex. At Rimer and Reason, we make things clear. Your success is our business.

> Compared to outlays, existing tax expenditures are subject to a less comprehensive management and reporting framework. This hampers the effective monitoring and scrutiny of individual tax expenditures. In many cases, it is not possible to show whether objectives are being achieved and whether benefits are proportionate to costs.

> Every day, in every bakery, Bakers Delight bakers create a range of traditional and gourmet breads.

The right vehicle for the wrong times.

To complete this quote you will need to know the rebuilding cost of your home. We have a calculator that can help you.

The only disappointment when you drive it is that you can't see it from the outside.

Spring reaches the summit of Kosciusko National Park at about the same time as the summer holidays. It's January before she moves above the treeline and sits to rest on the highest hill, apologising for her lateness by sending flowers.

If you're planning to have treatment in a private hospital, there's a quick way to make sure you won't have to cope with potentially thousands of dollars worth of unexpected bills. Check with us first to confirm that you're going to an Agreement hospital and that your planned treatment is covered and the usual conditions of your hospital cover, such as waiting periods, have been met.

Cool writing is frank, but humane. So it may be a bit beyond (or less than) cool to describe the nation's economy, as Access Economics did in their quarterly *Business Outlook* in January 2009, as 'buggered'. Fashionable maybe, but cool—no.

Cool is also useful: it cuts through cant and speaks with everyday grace and clarity. *Ethics at Work: A Guide to Advertising's Grey Areas*, a cool classic, demonstrates this well. Written by David Morris, BMF and the St James Ethics Centre, it uses the diction of intelligent speech to talk briefly, memorably, usefully and economically about something—how to behave in a free market—it is inherently hard to speak of without platitude, pomp and prolixity.

Here are its four chief subheads. Notice how these questions and short phrases grab your attention and focus it very specifically.

What are Ethics?

Why do Advertising Agencies Need a Code of Ethics?

How to Behave

The Code: What we Believe

Here's some of the language under a couple of those headings.

What are Ethics? Ethics are a system of moral principles that help us determine right from wrong, good from bad …

Why do Advertising Agencies Need a Code of Ethics? Our industry relies on trust. We need to act with integrity to gain trust—from our clients, colleagues, suppliers, consumers and our critics.

The bulk of the short document explains each of the items listed under 'The Code: What we Believe'. Even in summary, these values are clear because the writers had the courage to talk them trimly and tidily onto the paper.

Stand up for what you believe is right.

Honour all agreements.

Don't break the law. Don't bend the law.

Respect all people.

Compete fairly.

Look after your colleagues.

Think before you act.

Be honest.

Pompous writing is formal but disrespectful; stiff but imprecise;

impersonal; convoluted; abstract; general; judgmental. In business, professional, academic and political settings, people seem to go out of their way to avoid simplicity and humanity in their writing. It might be argued that this is because they're striving to remain objective, but it's possible to retain your objectivity along with your humanity; they're not mutually exclusive.

Here's some pomp from a telco, trying to reach out to its disgruntled customer base after a communications breakdown.

> We have a strong focus cross company on improving our customer service and are driving initiatives to deliver that improvement. We have also set new targets company wide in regards to how we handle complaints ... We understand that we need to earn your support going forward through the provision of enhanced customer service.

Here's a piece of pompous prose, from a nature magazine.

> No avicide myself and, indeed, not much of a wide-ranging aviphage, I had always assumed that the so-called glorious twelfth occurred only in August when the aristocratic victim of your matched pair of Churchills or Boss' or Purdies (or what have you at £12,000 a throw) is, of course, our only and uniquely indigenous bird, the red grouse.

These three pieces of bureaucratic pomp come from the same document (a strategic plan); there are plenty more where these came from. Notice how circuitously and obscurely it speaks; count the buzz words (technical, bureaucratic and managerial); notice the repetition (the department seems not to notice) of words such as 'support' and 'process', and, more understandably, but tiresomely, 'information' and, of course, 'identity'.

1. The department anticipates that the key deliverables will be progressed to the extent outlined below.

   By 2010 new and enhanced management business processes will be operational in support of:

- detention reception processing …
- application processing of the refugee and humanitarian and onshore protection caseloads
- citizen application processing …
- interactions with approved external Australian and international agencies.

2. The capability will be the interface to the department's system of record for all identity information. It will:

    - support the capture, storage and retrieval of identity information of the department's clients …
    - support searching for and identifying the department's clients using any or all of the following techniques …
    - interface with the Australian Government, international and commercial systems supporting the sharing and validation of identity information on the department's clients …

3. This initiative remains a core element to the identity management strategy and will be one of the most visible outcomes when it is fully implemented.

And, to close, some classic corporate pomp.

> By the conclusion of the workshop, participants will be fully equipped to enhance their performance in a range of management contexts, develop and build upon their current skillsets, embrace the range of tools, knowledge and techniques available to them and understand when, where and how to leverage these for optimum outcomes.

5 Clear/obscure

Clear writing has a point and makes it; it removes from its sentences everything that might occlude their meaning. It's focused and limpid. It delivers meaning without making its reader struggle; it starts making the sense it means to make at the start, and never stops.

You write obscurely when you write without having first got your thinking straight (when you begin before you arrive); when you're clear about what you mean but don't find a way to make your meaning plain; or, when you know what you mean and how to say that clearly, but abstain, or beat around the bush, with nothing like the clarity of that appealing Australian cliché.

In politically touchy situations, writers often work hard to make sure they can't be seen, under any circumstances whatsoever, to have committed themselves on paper to anything that might at some point in the foreseeable future come back to bite them. An understandable anxiety, but one to which a good writer won't surrender. If you feel constrained—if your boss is giving you the sign to pull your head in, if there's a danger of unnecessarily inflaming a tricky situation, or getting someone innocent into trouble, or tipping off your competitors, or of crashing the stock market—don't obfuscate. Try, at least, to leave your reader with a clear understanding of what it is you're not saying: because you can't yet, because the jury is still out, or the science is not in, or because it was outside your brief, or beyond the scope of the paper. Better still, work out what you are free to say clearly, and say that clearly. When Mark was a defamation lawyer, the word from the partners he worked with was: there's nothing you can't write (and stay out of trouble for having written) if you can just find a good defamation lawyer—or, failing that, if you have a good big dictionary, a calm mind, a cool hand, and a wise friend or two. Oh, and deep pockets.

Don't be arch; don't be snide; don't nudge and wink. It's a bad look, and it is certain to bite you back. Your readers are smarter than you think, and many of them have been around longer than you have; they know evasion when they see it.

Work out what you can be clear about and be very clear about it. If there are things you cannot say, don't say them.

Even if your intentions are honourable, if your writing is obscure, readers will presume that your commitment to full and frank disclosure is somewhat less than absolute.

Instead of

> A superior-quality learning environment is a necessary precondition for facilitation and enhancement of the ongoing learning process.

try

> Children need good schools if they are to learn effectively.

Or, though it may say something different

> Good schools teach students the art of learning.

Instead of

> If there are any points on which you require further explanation or more particulars we shall be glad to furnish such additional details as may be required by telephone.

Try

> If you have any questions, please phone.

None of this is to say a business or technical writer may not use unfamiliar language where it is the only way to say exactly what you mean. A subpoena is a 'subpoena' and an enjambment an 'enjambment' (though we could do with a definition) no matter how few people know what one is; syntax is 'syntax'; a urinary tract infection is 'a urinary tract infection'. Statistics, finance, law, genetics, econometrics, engineering, physics: these and other disciplines of thought and practice have their idioms—their specialised diction adapted to and useful for the instruments, activities and actions professionals in those fields have to deal with. Use such language, where you need to; but use it sparingly. Always favour the everyday word. Explain technicalities whenever you can't be sure everyone you're writing for will understand them; explain them most times, anyway—it's a good discipline of mind. And beware addiction; such language is an emblem of membership to a club, and our egos find it hard to wean themselves off the language that makes us feel like we belong.

Distinguish such technical idioms, which have their place, from managerial, bureaucratic and other forms of cliché, which do not. You don't have to call your approach a 'methodology', for instance; opposing camps, or more generally two elements of one whole (the city and the bush), don't have to be dubbed 'a binary'; a book, much less a painting, isn't by definition 'a text' or 'discourse'; strategies don't have to be 'implemented'; a new course doesn't have to be 'delivered'; a new project isn't required to be an 'initiative'; a new system needn't be described as a 'capability', nor a laboratory a 'facility'; 'end' will do for 'expiration'; and 'you should' is probably more effective than 'it is incumbent upon anyone in your position'.

The Little Red Writing Book draws the distinction between such 'verbal profundity' and the sparing use of apt technical expressions: see pp. 122 and 141.

6 Fluent/clunky

The best writing flows, and it hangs together; sentences follow each other, paragraphs follow paragraphs, in orderly sequence. Fluent prose states and—by exploration, explanation, argumentation, example, and persuasive language—makes its case. More than likely, it begins with its thesis, justifies it, and restates it.

The pyramid form in which journalists are taught to craft their stories has a lot to recommend it. Start with what the whole story comes down to; then detail the who, the what, the why, the when, the where, and the how. Then, if you've got time and space, for any reader who also has time and who cares, feel free to develop your thoughts at length, but make sure they're still relevant—and orderly. This approach imposes order on a piece of prose, and it's an order readers want: they get the key message up front, and they get to decide how much more they need or want to know.

We have more to say about the lead in 'The art of the start' in chapter 5.

Here are a couple of orderly paragraphs from the Stern Review of the economics of climate change. You know exactly where you stand and where you're being led next and why you're being led there. The shift of gear between paragraphs, from the local terrain of the report to the global terrain of the phenomenon, is managed by means of a short transitional sentence.

> The Review first examines the evidence on the economic impacts of climate change itself, and explores the economics of stabilising greenhouse gases in the atmosphere. The second half of the Review considers the complex policy challenges involved in managing the transition to a low-carbon economy and in ensuring that societies can adapt to the consequences of climate change that can no longer be avoided.
>
> The Review takes an international perspective. Climate change is global in its causes and consequences, and international collective action will be critical in driving an effective, efficient and equitable response on the scale required. This response will require deeper international co-operation in many areas—most notably in creating price signals and markets for carbon, spurring technology research, development and deployment, and promoting adaptation, particularly for developing countries.

Suboptimal prose, to borrow a suboptimal phrase, flows, too—but it flows all over the place. And it hangs—but it doesn't hang together. Sentences seem assembled at random; dot points abound; there may be a case but it won't be demonstrated; one paragraph follows another for no apparent reason. This can be, at best, frustrating for the reader and, at worst, downright dangerous for everyone concerned: through boredom, confusion or irritation, they may never get to the important bits. Time at work is too precious—eternity is too short—for anyone to want to spend it losing the thread of a badly made argument. So we stop. And rightly so.

It's easier to keep yourself and your reader on track if you know from the start what the track is, and where it's meant to be taking you. Look at what we say about planning and mindmapping in chapters 2 and 5.

Bad writing is a mess: disorderly, unkempt, repetitive, circular.

> We are able to provide the customer with a unique experience unlike anything they have ever seen before, due to our fastidious attention to detail, highly trained staff and our superior customer service.

> In the study conducted by an independent research firm, men responded that they are superior to women in problem solving, inspiring, delegating, and influencing upward. Women participants also affirmed this finding, explaining that they also internalised these beliefs into their leadership expectations. Contrary to the popular conviction that men make better leaders, it is proposed that leadership should be defined in terms of universal leadership characteristics, which include spirituality and transformational behaviours.

7 Finished/hasty

The more you work on a piece of writing, the better it mostly gets. It takes more drafts than you'd think to make a piece of writing that doesn't feel drafty—to produce a piece of copy that, paradoxically, feels natural and unaffected, as though it dropped from your lips like a cool and elegant speaking of your cool and elegant mind. You finish a piece of business writing not just by reaching your word limit, by running out of time or things to say. You finish it by drafting and redrafting, by sleeping on it and looking at it cold in the morning, and by rewriting until you're left with what you really meant to say in the first place—a document you'd be happy to see published and to read again in ten years' time in a court of law, a trim, carefully conceived and made, empathetic, cool, clear and fluent piece of functional prose.

Too much functional writing is only notionally finished; too many *draft* letters and reports, papers and theses and brochures are let out into the world as if they were pieces of writing: typos, spelling mistakes, broken logic, grammatical gaffes, pomposities, atrocities and most of the rest of it.

This is probably the most common mistake that people make, and it's easy to understand in the context of business, where deadlines are usually never far away, as opposed to writing for pleasure, where the act of writing is an end in itself. Not many of us have the luxury of being able to say, as Oscar Wilde once did, 'this morning, I wrote a sentence. Then, this afternoon, I deleted it.' It's possible that Wilde, prone to a little sassy overstatement, may have said that in jest, but his point stands: writing needs work, and sometimes you need to take out most of what you first put in. You need to put a thing the way it makes most sense for your reader, so that you can achieve your business end. Making sense fast means putting in some time; it means learning a healthy mistrust for the way you put things first time round.

The more writing you do, the better—and quicker—you'll get, but no one gets so good they get it right the first time. Thomas Mann, a great writer, once wrote that a writer is 'a man to whom the writing comes harder than to almost anyone else'—because, of all people who have to write, writers are the least easily satisfied with their first attempts.

Writing is by nature messy, hard and repetitive. It's rarely its best—or even passable—when you make it in a hurry. Finishing, in other words, takes time. (The words you're reading now have been through five drafts and an exacting copy-edit, and after all that a proofread.) So make sure you leave some time. And you needn't—you probably shouldn't—do it all on your own.

If you don't have the time or patience, or you don't think you have the skill, to finish your own writing, find someone who does. Ask a colleague to copy-edit your best shot at a final draft (it should be your third or fourth draft, if it's a document of any length or importance); but better still, since colleagues have their own work to do, hire a professional copy editor.

In the *New York Times* in 2008, Lawrence Downes wrote 'the copy editor's job, to the extent possible under deadline, is to slow down, think things through, do the math and ask the irritating question.' He was talking about newspaper publishing, and its decline in the face of increasing pressure from online news operations, but with a little paraphrasing, his words could apply to your writing at work: 'Copy editors handle the final transition to an ink-on-paper object ... they do the refining and packaging. They trim words, fix grammar, punctuation and style, write headlines and captions. But they also do a lot more. Copy editors are the last set of eyes before [the reader's]. They are more powerful than proofreaders. They untangle twisted prose. They are surgeons, removing growths of error and irrelevance; they are minimalist chefs, straining fat.' While he's right—copy editors are more powerful than proofreaders—don't think you can do without a final proofreading. It might just spare you the embarrassment of 'someone else's whore' (for 'shore', an easy typo to make; a meaning very different), or 'I think this calls for a pubic meeting' (an 'l' can make one hell of a difference).

Think of it as total quality management. Manufacturers learned a long time ago it's better to do whatever it takes to make sure only the best, most reliable product rolls off the production line than to cut corners and find yourself busier than you need to be processing returns and dealing with complaints. Substandard processes make substandard products; products that fall apart make businesses fall apart.

It's the same with writing; invest the time and skill, and even the money, it takes to get it right; practise the virtues and abstain from the vices, and you'll avoid the damage that faulty sentences cause. But it's not just about avoiding trouble; it's about doing some good, and not just to yourself—making sense always helps. It builds goodwill, it engenders loyalty, it spares the world the litter of faulty sentences and the rancour of their readers.

CHAPTER 4

THE BUSINESS-WRITING CANON

The document you have to write, whatever else defines and constrains it, is a piece of writing—and there's nothing much you don't know now about how to write anything, if you've read the first three chapters of this book. Write like you're talking about something you know to someone you trust; have a point and make it (and make it first); favour everyday words over commercial, academic, bureaucratic or other language; favour short words over long ones; mix up the length of your sentences; take more care but employ less formality than you're used to; don't parrot the lingo—write like an intelligent, independent-minded, cool and informed grown-up; write it the way you'd (really) like to read it; tell the story of the facts, and keep the story short; aim not to keep your reader a moment longer than necessary; write to sound like the kind of person or the kind of organisation you'd like to be (and be seen as); write to achieve, to get the business done; take more time (so that you save your reader time); vary the length of your sentences; put people in your sentences, and have them perform some verbs; keep your language as simple and unambiguous as you can; learn the seven heavenly virtues in chapter 3 and observe them even when it hardly seems to matter; question what you think they taught you at school; avert your eyes from most of the templates you'll be offered at work; fashion your own, instead, to suit your voice and reader and purpose; keep taking care; and just when you think you're finished, try one more draft. You should be right now; and if you don't think you will be, don't forget: you're not alone. There are copy editors out there waiting to help.

But though everything you write at work is a piece of writing to which the same wisdom always applies, let's take some documents from the business writing canon and workshop them. This chapter is a guide to twelve of the most commonly encountered varieties of business writing; it analyses the demands and constraints of some particular pieces of prose, and it shows you how to go about them better.

This book can't cover all the kinds of writing you're likely to face; nor does it have enough pages to offer templates for these documents. Even if it did, we wouldn't—not being especially passionate about templates (see chapter 1). There are other—fatter, less opinionated—books that do that. Good writers need to write things for themselves—schooled by good examples and guided by some good old, durable and memorable ideas. And that's the way we run this workshop. Just as a smart functional writer will know how to apply first principles to the writing challenge in front of her, so you should be able to cut and paste this analysis and apply what these days are called 'learnings'—or, better yet, 'key learning outcomes' or 'core deliverables'—to documents analogous to the ones we pick on here.

We can't be exhaustive, then, and we don't want to be prescriptive. But there are some key documents, and there are some particular things to say about them, some tricks to learn, some pitfalls to sidestep. Let's start with a model for writing anything.

A model for writing anything

Edward Bailey, who's written some good books about good business writing, proposes a model intended to help you write anything you have to write at work, from short memos to long reports. Its virtues are its simplicity and rigour—if you follow it, you won't go far wrong; and it will force you to write with focus and clarity. (Its vice is, it's a template; if you followed it religiously, your documents, though tidy, would probably sound formulaic.)

1. Begin the document (memo, report, letter) with your main point—why am I writing to you? Why has the report been commissioned and what has it found? And so on. Then support that with a little context and background. There's your first paragraph.
2. Then organise your content—the body of the document—into blocks of related information. Each may turn into just a paragraph or many pages.
3. Label each block with a heading or a topic sentence. Use subheadings if the sections become too long.
4. Begin each of those blocks with its main point. If your heading is a question, answer it in your first sentence.
5. Use detail, examples, research data, etc. to back up each main point.
6. At the end, ask for action, point the way ahead (after restating your purpose, if the document is long).

Here is a short proposal that employs the Bailey model.

> This memo asks for your authorisation to rent three computers for a total cost of $900.
>
> We have ordered three personal computers that we need for the Balmain project, but the supplier can't get them to us until 1 December. Because we must start the project sooner, we have a problem—we are three computers short for three months, and cannot afford to be. Renting is the most effective solution, for reasons I set out here.
>
> First, some background.
>
> **Why are the new computers late?**
> Although we placed orders in plenty of time, the supplier has run into

problems with defective computer chips. As a result ... [the memo goes on to outline the sequence of events and activities].

The options

Go to a fresh supplier

We could try to source computers elsewhere. Bob has looked into this. There are a number of problems:

- This [we leave out the detail]
- That
- The other thing.

Short-term rental

The alternative is to rent the computers we need for the three months. After investigating this option with a few companies, I discovered that the best terms available are ...

Recommendation—we lease three computers

My recommendation is that we hire the computers we need from Apple Inc. ...

Decision

Because of the pressing need for the computers, I would appreciate your decision as soon as possible. Can I suggest that we settle this at our meeting tomorrow morning?

1 Letters

No one writes letters anymore. No one except everyone in business, that is—selling us something, outlining something, offering us the job, letting us go, justifying or advertising some political action, inviting some public comment.

Letters are an intimate discourse: through many centuries, before anyone thought of the telephone, the telegraph, email or Twitter, the letter was how people conversed when distance separated them—lovers with their beloved, mothers with their children, a brother in the colonies with his sister back in London, Beatrix Potter in the Lakes District with her friends' children in London, soldiers in Flanders with their families on the station back home. Though it's true that letters have also been used by Caesars in Rome to send orders to their generals in Gaul and by prophets to send guidance to their flocks in Ephesus, letters mostly travelled between kith and kin and spoke familiarly—with respect and affection. Letters, through history, have let people speak on paper the way they would have spoken face to face, if they could. They've enabled intimacy when distance precluded it.

Jane Austen wrote letters. So did Henry James. So did the people they wrote about. And hardly any of the letters were for business. They were for family, for love, for duty.

Letters belong, then, to relationships of trust; where they don't, they presume, anticipate and try to establish relationships of trust. That's why they start with something like 'Dear' and end with something like 'Yours' or 'Faithfully', often both. History explains those personal endearments and protestations of loyalty.

Which are beginning to sound odd these days, even though they stick, when all the people who once wrote 'Dear' to people who were dear to them now send texts and emails instead, and the only people who send letters and write 'Dear' in them are business people, who often send them to people towards whom they don't feel dear at all.

To put a letter to a business use, given the intimacies that have attended the long history of the epistle, is already to stretch a point. 'Business letter' should be an oxymoron. And yet letters have been part of business discourse—the very heart of it until recently—for a very long time. Now, though most business is transacted electronically or in person, letters are still central; indeed, no one much else sends them anymore, except people doing their jobs.

In every era over their long history, good letters, business or personal, probably adopted a tone at the formal end of natural. Jane Austen and her characters wrote letters in the respectful but conversational idiom of the day. Don't ape their now antique style—mirror, instead, their attitude. Old letters from that epistolary era were respectful. But because they were vessels for trust, friendship, love, attachment, they weren't stuffy; they were personable. And so it should still be with letters, including business letters. Remember the intimate—the conversational and personal—history of the letter, no matter what the letter has to say; no matter who you think they should think you are and whom you're writing for. Write as informally as you feel able, less formally than you feel you must. Write letters like everything else, in fact: more naturally, but more carefully than you've probably been doing it. Do your politics off the paper; on the paper, talk tidily. Be sincere; be faithful; be done.

It may be that business letters have become more formal since everyone else stopped writing them except the busy and serious people doing serious business; it may be they've grown stiffer since all the intimate discourse migrated to email and Facebook and Twitter. But there's no reason for the stiffness—there's reason, in fact, for familiarity. In truth, letters are nothing but emails on paper, for the email is the new intimate discourse. Letter writers would do well to write letters the way the best writers write emails—with the kind of care, and the kind of conversational turn of phrase that once characterised letters.

Like this email, for example.

Hi, Maureen.

Nice to hear from you after all these months. It's good to get your news and hear of your plans.

If you were coming through next Sept., I could most certainly arrange a reading and accommodation. We may all be out of work by then, due to the economy, so that's about all I can promise for now. But it could work. I would also suggest that you apply for a residency at the Volcano Arts

Center in the Volcanoes National Park. They don't have much money, but they are right in the park and provide a lovely quiet place—unless the volcano explodes, of course. Did you visit there?

I just received another of those generic invitations to a conference, which I would have ignored except that it's in Sydney. I'll attach it below. If you were interested or able, I'm thinking we could cobble together a few friends to present a colloquium or panel on international writing, the ethical imagination—something of that sort. I won't even consider it unless you were involved from that end. Just a thought.

Or maybe it's just a money-making fraud.

Be well, friend,
Frank

You'd use a letter, as opposed to sending an email or making a call, when you have something of particular importance to communicate—not just a step in the process; you might use a letter for

- a job application or offer
- a resignation
- a bid
- advice to a client
- letting a tender
- a plea or complaint to council.

But there are few rules. We use email so much these days that nearly every piece of business communication is transacted that way. Where letters are still used, they are frequently sent by email—as emails themselves or as attachments to emails. In the end, it's not the form or the mode of transmission that counts; it's how well the piece of writing addresses its reader, its subject and its purpose.

Here are some tips for writing letters.

1 Plan and structure your letters before you start. Don't just start. Use a quick mindmap (see chapter 5 of *The Little Red Writing Book*) to derive your main issues and work out a clearheaded way of saying why you're writing.

2 Call to mind these questions, and set down answers before you start.
   - What do I want to say?
   - What do I want to achieve?
   - Whom am I writing to, what is their attitude and what do they know?
   - What is my attitude to what I have to say and what I want to achieve? (If you're anxious or angry or proud, acknowledge it, and set that feeling aside. Good writing doesn't want to betray your emotions; good writing tells the story of the facts.)
   - Is a letter the best way to go? (Would you be better off phoning, or calling on the person, or sending an email?)

3 Use a main heading to establish the territory the letter covers. Be as specific as you can. Avoid recitals of reference numbers and account details. If you want to, use subheadings to flag your main points. Nothing precludes headings, even in a letter. Do whatever you need to do to make your message clear and coherent.

4 Don't start with recitals of company or government policy or business objectives; start by announcing why you're writing. Think about the questions on a reader's mind as they open your letter, and answer them: why are they writing to me; what's this about; how does it concern me; what do they want me to do? Get, in other words, straight to the point: 'I write to invite you to become a Friend of the Festival.'

5 Forget about flabby, bureaucratic expressions at the start, like 'With reference to' and 'Further to'. Where is it written that a letter must begin that way? Don't waste so important a sentence as the first on

bureaucracy. Name your topic and start talking about it. Make a link to the letter, conversation or meeting that came before, if something did; but do it elegantly and more like you would in conversation. Try 'I have read your letter and would like to suggest …' or 'Thank you for your letter' or 'In your letter, you ask about …' or 'When we met last week, you inquired …'—that sort of thing.

6 Apply all the usual rules of good style: be concrete; be trim; be active; be humane and real; vary your sentences in length and structure, and at the very least make sure each of them makes the sense you mean it to make.

7 A letter is as long as it needs to be, but no longer. If it needs to be long, keep it tidy—with subheadings and well-ordered sentences.

8 Point the way ahead. Leave the reader knowing what you want to happen next, what you will do next, and what, if anything, they need to do.

9 Don't feel obliged to finish with 'Should you have any further questions, please do not hesitate to contact myself …'. If you want to invite them to call you, be more straightforward: 'Please call me if I can help you further.' But it isn't compulsory; indeed, it is clichéd, as we'll discuss later, to close in this way. And, although it probably feels like the polite thing to do, it even implies you may not have bothered or managed to make yourself sufficiently clear in the paragraphs above. Try something like this: 'I hope this letter answers your questions about the new policy'; 'I look forward to having you on board.'

10 Greetings. Despite attempts to replace it with 'Good morning' and 'Hi' and 'Greetings', 'Dear' still rules. Whether you use the title (Dr, Professor, Mrs, Ms, Mr) and family name or given name, or go for 'Dear Sir' or 'Dear Madam' depends on your judgment about the form of address your reader will feel comfortable with, how well you know them, and whether you actually know their name. As a general rule, favour the least formal approach. Few people expect to

be addressed as 'Sir' or 'Madam' or by title and family name after the initial approach, or if you know them. There are few rules anymore, and undue formality can sound distant and pompous. Don't forget: you're allowed to follow your own etiquettes; this is your letter, after all.

Although American writers often address a reader (before they know them, generally) as, for example, 'Dear Charles Rigby' or even 'Dear Dr Charles Rigby', that sounds strange in Australia. Here, as in the rest of the former British Commonwealth, it's either 'Dear Charles' or 'Dear Dr Rigby'. Don't ask us why. And don't be surprised if it changes while you're out to lunch one day.

11 Sign-offs. Convention still favours 'Yours sincerely' (if you've opened with 'Dear Ms Lim') and 'Yours faithfully' (with 'Dear Madam'). But this convention is weakening. You may close with 'Best regards', 'Regards', 'Best wishes', 'With thanks', 'Sincerely', or some such, if that sits comfortably with you.

12 Avoid 'Dear homeowner/resident/customer/parent/ASLE member' if you can. No one reads a letter as though they were such a category; they read as themselves. And if you've had anything to do with direct marketing, you'll know that this is a big turn-off. So find a way to put their name in the letter.

13 Read it again, and again, before you print and send it. Sleep on it, perhaps, and look at it fresh tomorrow. (See 'No—we're *not* there yet' in chapter 2.)

2 Emails

Write letters more like emails and emails more like letters. From the email, a letter writer could learn to relax; from the letter, the emailer could learn to take care.

If a letter is best tackled as an email on paper, an email is best tackled as a letter on screen. Go about it the way Frank did in the email to his friend about the conference above.

When you think about it, it hardly matters how the message is transmitted: it's a piece of writing. All the usual writing rules apply.

The medium *hardly* matters, but it matters a bit.

1 Take good care. Unlike letters, emails arrive almost the moment we send them, and this immediacy can make them feel like conversations. This may be why we write them less formally—and largely that's a good thing. But there's a downside: emails feel so much like talking and so little like writing to some writers that they forget to take the care that writing demands. Writing isn't merely talking—it's talk *tidied*. A hasty thought, careless diction, sloppy syntax, typos and grammar gaffes, sentences that drop their bundle, shouting or sniggering belong no better in an email than in an annual report or a thesis.

   So forget that your email is an email; think of it as a piece of writing, and write it with all the usual care.

   Email makes things happen fast; it allows great economies of time. Think how long it used to take to conduct the average negotiation with a potential supplier or buyer in snail mail. Speed is addictive, though. It engenders impatience—emailers tend to expect an almost immediate response to their emails, whereas they'd wait weeks for a reply to their letter. Don't rush your writing; it's false economy. Let your writing take as long as writing needs to take. Don't feel obliged to dash off a reply while the electrons are still buzzing in your inbox; that can lead to all sorts of regrets. Read it, digest it, go for a walk, sleep on it if you must; one way or another, consider your response and craft it, as though it were a piece of writing. You don't have to write an email hastily just because you can send it at speed.

   A tip: compose emails that really matter as Word documents; paste them into an email when they're good to go. This can help you get out of that hectic email state of mind; it also gives you access to the spelling and grammar checkers not always available in email programs. In short, to make it the best email it can be, don't *write* it as an email; just *send* it as an email.

2 Don't go on. If all good business writing should be trim, emails should be even trimmer. Emails fly: they come fast, and they expect speedy replies. And emails get read onscreen, and screens are smaller than pages and harder to read. So don't go on. Start with the main point, and stick with it. Then stop.

If you have more to say than will fit on a screen (generally less than a page), stop and think before you start to write. You'll need to give the email some shape, and you'll need to paint the big picture first; you should then foreshadow the ground the rest of the email will cover.

If you have a lot to say, it may be better to make a Word document of your argument or exposition, or whatever it is, and attach that to a short email that summarises the attachment.

If you have several points to make, send a separate email for each of them (though this may clog your reader's inbox); commonly, if you send an email about three or four separate matters, you get a reply that deals with only one or two of them. We read and respond to emails hastily. Expect this, and control for it.

3 Get your reader's attention and focus their mind with a clear and engaging subject line. And try to spell it correctly—there's nothing worse than rereading your typo when you get the reply.

Mark's inbox at the moment has emails with these subject lines: 'Invoice for Writing the Real', 'Thoughts on last night's meeting', 'Request to give a reading', 'Upstairs/downstairs', 'Location reminder', 'Class confirmation, Business Writing—please reply to this email', 'Sale of 23 Wingello Street'.

Those are all good. Avoid subjects full of numbers, like 'Account number 56739999-0998'.

Name what you're selling, what you're saying, what you're responding to. But you don't have to encapsulate the whole message.

Although it will sometimes work to leave the original sender's subject line intact in your reply, it's better to coin something that indicates how your email is linked to the one it relates to: 'Your proposal—my response'.

4 Every letter addresses its reader as 'Dear', but there are more options in an email:

- Dear Pip
- Pip
- Hi/Hey
- Hi, Vikram/Hey, Vikram (or, if you like, 'Hi Vikram/Hey Vikram').

Another option is nothing at all. That needn't be rude, even if your email opens the conversation; the name of the recipient is in the address line at the top of the email, so arguably it's redundant to name them again. Though some readers may expect their name and take its absence as a sign of rudeness, a good writer relies less on formalities and more on how they make their sentences to establish their tone. There's nothing unfriendly in itself about the absence of a salutation; there is always something unfriendly about unfriendly prose.

It's more likely you'll drop the salutation once a couple of emails have travelled back and forth, or if you know the recipient well. It used to be conventional to drop the greeting and the name from office memos, when such things were still sent. These days there's a kind of email that serves as a memo (generally notifying more than one recipient of some event or information or change of procedure), and it would be apt to drop the greeting for those.

You're more likely to get an email addressing you as 'Dear' when the writer doesn't know you or is opening the conversation with you.

But, then again, we have friends and colleagues who email us as 'Dear Mark' or 'Dear Geoff', even though they know us well. There are writers for whom an email remains a fast kind of letter, and it's hard to argue with their logic.

There is, in other words, no single protocol. You have choices.

When an email is sent to many people, especially too many to name in the greeting, the best approach is no salutation at all. 'Hi, all' is common, but illogical. No reader is 'all': emails are not read by a crowd; each reader reads the email separately. If you can't readily put each reader's name on each reader's email, try just starting. You'll get used to it. Where the email asks one particular person to do something, make that clear in the body copy.

5 Close. If you start, 'Dear Arundhati', you may think of closing with 'Yours sincerely'. That is the old letter etiquette. If you start with 'Hi', you'd be unlikely to go with 'Yours sincerely'; more likely 'Best' or 'See you soon' or 'Talk to you Monday' or 'See you in New York in May' or 'Take care' or 'Regards' or 'Cheers', or even nothing. No form has had a chance to settle in, and we suspect it won't. Email is a much looser and newer technology than letter. Again, with freedom comes responsibility; enjoy the freedom, but be aware of the context. You would no sooner send an email to your beloved commencing with 'My Dearest Prudence' and ending with 'Respectfully yours' than you would offer policy advice to your departmental secretary topped and tailed with 'Yo, Bro' and 'Chill', respectively.

6 Everyone gets more work emails than they'd like, so don't copy in anyone who doesn't really need to know. Be sparing—remember how many redundant emails land in your inbox, and how they keep you from noticing or even reading the emails that really do require your attention. The test might be whether you'd actually mention the matter to the person in question.

Think the same way about forwarding emails. It's good manners to forward only those emails where the sender has asked you to do that, or has given you permission, or where that permission is implicit. If in doubt, ask the author if she minds.

7 Another matter of email etiquette is the use of the Urgent flag. Don't use it—unless your message really is urgent. You've heard of the little boy who cried wolf, no doubt; perhaps more than once. But if it's that urgent, don't rely on an email alone: call or text, or if they're in the same building, go knock on their door.

3 Reports

Reports are like any other kind of writing—only longer.

And the main challenge in writing reports comes from their length. In a report (not unlike a book), you need to cover a lot of ground, marshal a lot of material. Organising everything—first your material, then yourself, then your ideas, and finally your document—becomes even more important and even harder to master than it always is. Reports are a structural challenge, above all. Everything keeps getting away from you; its hard to remember everything; it's harder still to keep your point in mind under the weight of all the detail (especially if you neglected your mind-map at the outset); it's easy, on the other hand, to repeat yourself; and you need to work at pacing your argument and exposition—saying things in the right order, relating everything to everything else.

More on structure in a moment. First, a little on voice and diction. A report is less personal than a letter—you don't send a report to your son or your lover. But a report is a piece of writing—so it needs to be clear, and, like all writing, it'll go best if it sounds like a spoken thing. There's no need to make it dry or formal—reports don't have to be dull; they have to be, above all, clear.

Clarity, care and humanity are the guiding principles. You're still talking; and your talk should be tidier than ever; but you'll probably want to avoid endearments, jokes and wisecracks. It's hard to sign off on a policy recommendation when you're laughing so hard you've got tears in your eyes. This is writing we're talking about, so it's still an act of speech performed on paper; it's still personal—but not that personal. Not as personal as an email or a letter, anyway. There's room for a human voice, but it will maintain a little distance; it will be a bit reserved.

On account of their length, and the amount of time you ask a reader to spend inside them, there's an argument that a report, of all the documents you write, should be the most like a piece of tidied talk—in the manner of a good book (since a book is what a report most resembles). Write a report the way Darwin speaks *The Origin of Species*, for instance; the way Stern speaks his report on climate change.

Don't try to affect what you imagine to be a report writer's tone. Imagine yourself, if you can, as a literate scientist. Tell the story of the facts as they presented themselves to you. You set aside your tastes and biases; you apply scientific, dispassionate measures; you look with disinterest (which means neutrality; more on this later) at the findings your approach yields; you draw conclusions logically, not emotionally; you propose solutions suggested by the experts in the literature. What you happen to think is irrelevant. This is the theory, anyhow.

Reports come in many kinds and run to various lengths, but they're rarely short. They involve research and analysis; they generally draw conclusions and reach a finding or make a case or a bunch of recommendations. They are hard to summarise, but summarising them is the key to their success.

Scientists write reports when they write up the process and findings of their experiments. IT consultants write reports when they give existing and prospective clients needs analyses. Doctors write reports on their patients. Coroners write reports on the dead; environmental consultants write environmental assessments—those are reports, too. Companies write annual reports for their shareholders and for the markets. Journalists file reports. Management consultants write reports of their analysis of client business operations. Teachers write reports. Auditors write audit reports. Committees write reports for governments. A thesis, too, is a species of report.

What all these documents have in common is a methodical approach: you take (and outline) a scenario (problem, objective, field of operations, illness, story); sometimes you propose a hypothesis about that matter and set out to test it, but in any event, you look very hard, rigorously and objectively at the matter; you apply, specifically, a method of analysis to the problem or scenario (you gather relevant data, you measure it, you conduct all manner of relevant research in order to test your hypothesis); you make some findings (what you discover when you apply those tests and measures); you interpret those findings logically and draw conclusions; you make some recommendations or draw out the implications and point the way ahead. Your report documents your approach—a model drawn from science but applied well beyond it.

Some reports are nowhere near as exact and exacting—still, they are all a sustained and objective kind of looking and telling. Reports, one way or another, communicate the results of research and reflect upon those results critically. Usually, a report proposes a course of action in response to its analysis of the research findings: a course of action such as a change in behaviour, procedure, strategy or legislation to resolve a problem identified.

With all this analysis to do, and findings to get right and recommendations (often sensitive and sometimes unwelcome) to craft, and supporting evidence and argumentation to marshal, it's hard to keep your story running, and your readers running with it, in a report. But it's vital. You must sift your data and make sense of it for your readers. Don't give them all the facts—only those material to the issue. Superfluous facts are as blinding—not to mention as dull—as science.

Reports vary widely, but here is a workable and conventional template.

1. Executive summary—encapsulates the whole report; allows a reader to get the whole report at a gulp, without needing to read it: thesis or conclusion; reasons; implications; summary of findings and recommendations.
2. Introduction—summarises the issue or problem, its background and context, why it matters, why you're looking into it and the scope of the inquiry.
3. Approach (perhaps part of the introduction)—explains your methodology, models, ways of sorting data. How you worked.
4. Findings (this will make up the bulk of your report, and you can organise it in many different ways)—lists the critical things you found when you applied your approach to the facts at hand. In this section you distil the critical facts you discovered and you say what they mean—you draw conclusions about them, pointing out the implications of the findings for the problem you were investigating and the context in which you looked. You anticipate the solutions you'll articulate next.
5. Recommendations—sets down the steps you propose to deal with the diagnosis you make in your findings. This is a report, so these are not, and should not be articulated as, your personal opinion.
6. Conclusion—wraps it all up and suggests what will happen next.

So to summarise, a strong introduction/abstract/summary is vital, as is a strong conclusion. The introduction should build on the title and help the reader to get their bearings, summarising the conclusion and highlighting the key points that are covered in greater depth further on in the document. And don't just copy selected sentences or paragraphs from the body of the document; that's boring, and sends messages like 'lazy' and 'patronising'—not good for the corporate image. The conclusion is your opportunity to reinforce your key message and, where appropriate, issue your call to action. Again, resist the temptation to copy material from the body of your document; say it in a new way, but make sure you don't contradict or muddy the message.

Because of the length of reports, it's impossible to compare how good and—let's call them suboptimal—reports go about these elements, but let's sample a few sentences and paragraphs.

Here's an example of a clear sentence.

> The paper identifies the key design decisions that are required, discusses alternative approaches to dealing with the key questions to be resolved, and indicates preferences among options.

Here's another one.

> Globalisation, demographic and structural shifts, resource issues, increasing demands and a dampening of economic growth all present significant challenges.

Here's a nice way to start an introduction.

> Economic growth is supposed to deliver prosperity. Higher incomes should mean better choices, richer lives, an improved quality of life for us all. That at least is the conventional wisdom. But things haven't always turned out that way.

And here's another.

> The Movement Alert List (MAL) is a computer database maintained by the Department of Immigration and Citizenship (DIAC) to protect the country from those people who may pose a threat to the Australian community. MAL is used to inform decisions about visa and citizenship grant and admission of non-citizens into the country. Checking takes place at several points, contributing to a 'layered' approach to border management. In this way, MAL forms an important element in Australia's national security and border protection strategy.

4 Executive summaries

Executive summaries don't stand alone—though you should write them so they can. They've become a vital part of most (larger) business documents these days. Executive summaries appear at the front of most business and bureaucratic reports. They're widely used in scholarship, too: an abstract of a conference paper, journal article or dissertation is an instance of an executive summary.

The purpose of the summary is to spare a reader the whole report. So a good summary, though it belongs to the report, should be complete and self-contained, sufficient unto itself, effectively a discrete document; a bad summary, on the other hand, will force you to read the whole report to make sense of what the summary fails to say clearly on its own. For this reason, and because they're so important, we'll treat the executive summary as though it were a document.

A summary, to borrow some business idiom, should add value—not just length—to a report. The specific value it adds is to say very clearly and very briefly what the longer document amounts to. The other value it adds is summary. Summarising has always been a valued writing skill, but the talent for it is not very evenly distributed. Writing is hard work, and summarising may be the hardest part of it. The executive summary, so called, seems to have been a coinage of the Second World War; General Eisenhower, so the story goes, won the war in the Pacific, admittedly not single-handedly, using one-page summaries of complex strategic plans.

So a reader gets from a good summary the gist of 80 pages in five; a good summary tells in short the story the report tells in full. In most business and even academic contexts, what a summary says should be enough, as the opening paragraph or two of a news story is, for the majority of readers. It should invite them to stop reading (or, if they feel they want the chapter and the verse, to jump into the report confident of where it's going to lead them). You will have succeeded, in other words, if most of your prospective readers never read your report or paper, but grasp its meaning from your summary.

Good summaries encapsulate a report without presuming the reader knows the meaning of key terms explained, and details explored, in the report; good summaries leave out none of the report's material elements; they include its key findings, its conclusion and its recommendations.

At the same time, because summaries are meant to be short and to add value (the value of paraphrase and explication), a good summary will reproduce relatively little copy from the report. Instead, it will paraphrase economically all the key findings and, to borrow another little bit of business-speak, the bottom line.

It is common these days to find executive summaries of ten pages—sometimes of forty or fifty—in reports, especially reports written in the public sector. No matter how complex the subject matter and how lengthy the report, however, a long executive summary is a contradiction in terms. So, how long should an executive summary be? One school of thought says that an executive summary should never run longer than a single page. General MacArthur and Winston Churchill, who coined and relied on the modern executive summary in the Second World War, insisted on this; the idea was to be able to see the whole thing at once. That rule, good for wartime leaders, probably has more merit in the age of the laptop than it did in the 1940s; keep your summary, if you can, to the size of a screen. But not too much harm will be done if you break it by a page or two. More than five pages will be too many, though—unless your report runs to hundreds of pages on a matter of national or global significance, in which case, keep it to ten pages tops.

Summaries often grow too long because they aren't really summaries—they're cut-and-pastes of key findings and recommendations, and they include too much narration of background and methodology. You can't fit a report into a summary unless you erode it to the least thing it can be and still be itself: to its essence.

One trick with recommendations, which are often many, is not to list them, certainly not verbatim, but to say that the report makes fifty (or however many) recommendations, and then briefly describe their nature and their purpose.

Although—perhaps because—summaries are short, how they are made matters: structure is a bigger deal in a summary even than it is in a report; you have no space for abstractions and polysyllabic waffle; you need to make the complex simple; you'll need some examples; you need to state your whole case, in skeletal form. Here's a summary of the recommendations we made to a client recently on how to improve their executive summaries.

1 Limit all summaries to three pages. (You could allow a further two pages under special circumstances, but a strict and strictly enforced page limit is more likely to force the changes of structure and style required.)

2 Begin each summary with a lead—a paragraph, at most two, that says what the study looked at, why and how, what it found, how much and why that matters (and by implication or specifically, what the report recommends). (See pages 52 to 53 for more leads.) The opening paragraph(s) should do, in other words, what a lead does in a good piece of journalism. The executive summary is the lead to the whole report, but the lead, itself, needs a lead: the lead paragraph summarises the summary. If the lead is not right at the start, it must be near the start (and certainly on the opening page).

   Here are a couple of good leads.

   What you call great music we call company policy.

   Researchers have found that watching too much television can shorten your life.

   This, by contrast, is not a good lead. It's way too general; it leaves out the detail you need if you're going to put it to any use.

The report that follows outlines the findings and recommendations of an inquiry that was conducted into green office procurement across the public sector. It contains a wide range of initiatives for agencies to consider in improving performance within a more sustainable office environment.

3 Adopt language (diction and style) that is plain, clear, concrete and specific.

4 Write descriptions of your objective, conclusion and recommendations (in summary) that avoid bland and generic language, such as: 'the objective of this study is to assess the effectiveness of …', 'the report found that there was significant scope for the agency to improve', and 'the report makes a number of recommendations aimed at improving the effectiveness …'. Because such wording can be used in any and every report, it gives poor value to a reader of any particular audit summary: it is equally generic and unhelpful in all reports. What precisely and actually are the issue, problem, and solution here? Phrase these key elements of the summary to address these questions squarely. Try, instead, something like this: 'this report concludes that the department failed in its duty of care in these two cases—a failure that resulted from systemic cultural factors and inadequate information management. It makes ten recommendations aimed at engendering cultural change, and operational improvements, specifically the development of IT systems adequate to the challenges of increasing levels of immigration and international travel.'

Ethics at Work, which we quoted from and discussed in chapter 3, starts with a one-page summary of the document, a code of ethics for the advertising industry. 'This guide is to help people working in advertising agencies do the right thing…', it begins. It then defines 'ethics' and lists the ten ethical principles the code spells out. That's an effective summary.

5 Characterise the *nature*, as well as the purpose, of recommenda-

tions: the nature, not the number—the quality, not the quantity—of recommendations is what matters. Don't feel obliged to paste in the summary the recommendations as you wrote them in full in the report; paraphrasing them neatly is more useful to a reader. Include cross-references to the full recommendations, if you like.

6 Dedicate no more than three paragraphs to background, history and context; dedicate one paragraph to your methodology; and run these paragraphs after, not before, the lead paragraph.

7 Use reader-oriented subheadings: What the Audit Looked At and What it Concluded; The Agency/Issue; Audit Issue and Audit Objective; What the Audit Examined.

Here are the first two paragraphs of a reasonably clear executive summary.

> The Australian Government has a large environmental footprint. In 2007–08 it procured over $26 billion of vehicles, office supplies, ICT, energy, waste and water services, office buildings and facilities and other goods and services. Consuming these goods and services to perform the activities of government, the public sector produces high levels of waste and emissions, and the Government is committed to reducing its environmental footprint. An audit conducted by the ANAO in 2005–06 concluded that sustainable procurement and office management practices had not been integrated into government operations; the audit made a number of recommendations to remedy that.
>
> The current audit, based on a survey of 63 agencies, assessed the progress made by the Government sector toward reducing its environmental footprint, particularly in procurement; consumption of paper and other consumables, IT and vehicles; water and waste management; energy use; and the efficient use of buildings. It also assessed progress on sustainability reporting. The audit concluded that while there are more examples of sustainable practices now than in 2005, there remains a wide disparity of performance across agencies, from very poor to best practice; notwithstanding progress made in particular agencies, the public sector as a whole has a lot of work yet to do to achieve its goal of being at the forefront of green procurement. In

particular, the audit found that agencies needed to develop integrated sustainability frameworks.

This one works all right, too, covering complicated territory.

> This audit reviews the completeness, quality and currency of the data maintained by the Department of Immigration and Citizenship (DIAC) on its Movement Alert List (MAL). MAL is two linked databases, the first (PAL), a list of persons who may pose a threat to Australia's s security, the second (DAL), primarily a list of stolen travel documents. As travel to and from Australia continues to grow, the number and complexity of records on MAL grows too; clearly it is essential to national security that the department maintain the accuracy and currency of the data on MAL, a challenging task as the size of the database grows and travel increases, a point emphasized by a number of reviews of MAL.
>
> This audit found that, while DIAC has grown the database, and used it successfully in its decision-making, the department has struggled to maintain the completeness, quality and currency of the information stored there, and the overall quality of the data has declined in recent years. The audit identified some shortcomings in the oversight of data entry; the need for a more strategic approach to the inclusion of Australian citizens on MAL; and the need for a review of the compliance of MAL with privacy laws. The audit makes five recommendations aimed at improving the quality of data on MAL by attention to these and other matters.

That executive summary, and the report it summarised, used some wonderfully clear, reader-oriented subheadings. These headings often do more than describe the territory of the paragraphs that follow; they summarise the conclusion those paragraphs reach. By all means try versions of these in your summaries:

- MAL is a central element in border protection
- Why it is important that DIAC manages MAL data well
- Conclusion—the completeness, quality and currency of MAL data are enduring problems for DIAC

- Conclusion—DIAC could improve controls over access to MAL
- PRIVACY—what agencies are required to do.

This abstract of an econometrics seminar arrived one day by email. It's about as short, clear, smart and engaging as an abstract or executive summary can get.

> Bank failures come in waves: one bank collapse is both cause and effect of many others. This is how it's been in the current crisis; this is how it has been historically. In the United States, there have been about 30 bank failures so far this year; the FDIC announces a few more each week. Instead of looking at the risks for individual financial institutions, regulators are focusing on macro-prudential regulation: looking at the financial system as a whole, measuring the aggregation of risks across the entire system; and allowing for linkages and interactions between individual banks. In this paper, we look at the failure of just one bank, the Penn Square Bank of Oklahoma, a small bank that collapsed in 1976 and brought down two major banks, Continental Illinois and Seattle First National. Penn Square was the Lehman Brothers of the 1980s.

Here's another example. A little bureaucratic diction ('prior to' and 'minimised') taints it, but that's a small matter compared to the elegance of thought and the general clarity of its expression.

> Prior to 7 February the State Government devoted unprecedented efforts and resources to informing the community about the fire risks Victoria faced. That campaign clearly had benefits, but it could not, on its own, translate levels of awareness and preparedness into universal action that minimised risk on the day of the fires. Indeed, no campaign will have universal success. The effectiveness of any campaign depends on the quality of information, the modes of dissemination and the willingness and capacity of people to hear, understand and act on the message. This is a shared responsibility between government and the people.

5 Website copy

Websites position you—digitally. They are the shopfront of today. They're marketing brochures in digital format, and they are often an organisation's first contact with its customers. They tell readers not just what you do but who you are and how you go about whatever it is you go about. They do this, of course, as much through the graphics as the words. But the words are vital, as words always are, and they need to be chosen with some awareness of what works and what doesn't on the net—and of the expectations and needs of onscreen readers.

Websites need to entertain, or at least engage, more than they need to inform. If they fail, the reader won't waste much time; one click, and they're gone. The medium is essentially visual, and readers expect a pleasing visual experience—even more than they do from a brochure or a book. So don't let your words get in the way—of a cool and memorable digital experience of you and what you stand for, of the aesthetic your website embodies and attributes to you.

We've said from the start here that all good writing has a human voice; that it's trim and vivid; that it's precise but not dull; that it alludes to the real world, not to the abstract realm. All this is more than ever true of writing for the web, in part because of the limitations of the single screen, in part because of the infotainment websites must deliver.

This little black book isn't going to try to show you how to design a website: visual design, in particular web design, is not our expertise—though, like you, we know what we like when we see it. Find a good web designer, and make sure they get who you really are. But since you'll probably end up writing the copy for your site, here are some things you should know.

1 Avoid slabs of text. We've already talked about keeping your reader in mind, and here's the thing about online readers; they don't so much read as look. Keep your paragraphs short; use dot points; use deft and

catchy headings and subheadings; incorporate photographs, graphs and other graphics. If you want to offer up wordy content (Mark's website lets readers sample his essays and poems, for instance), give a reader a short summary and a link they can click, if they choose, to read the full text (or print it out).

To use a business cliché, in an appropriate way for a change, readers should be given the opportunity to drill down according to their needs and interests. This means, of course, that you need to put a fair bit of thought into the structure of your website, just as you do with the structure of any piece of writing. It needs to feel intuitive, or at least logical, which won't always mean the same thing to all of your readers; and everything—all your links and moving images and whatnot—needs to work properly. There are few things more frustrating than links that transport you to strange and unexpected places or to nowhere at all.

And don't let graphical wizardry overwhelm content; try to keep the astonishment factor to a bare minimum.

2 Never stop talking. Copy in the ether must never lose its voice. In the digital world, we talk, even more than we do on paper. The worst websites are often those that have simply taken all their existing hard-copy documents and thrown them up on their website as PDFs without taking the trouble to provide an eye-catching showcase in this new (online) context. So work harder than ever, not just to keep your writing trim, but to make it sound like some bright person talking easily. Write your side of a terrific conversation.

3 Tell a story. Don't enumerate your accomplishments, client base, product lines, specialisations, in the usual way; don't write 'in this capacity we have the overall oversight of …' or anything like the hackneyed language in which we often write job descriptions and positioning statements on paper (don't do it there, either). Think of the way writing pulls you into a place or a character in a novel, a

memoir, a travelogue or a documentary, and try to tell your business story that way. Like this, maybe:

> Skype is software that enables the world's conversations. Millions of individuals and businesses use Skype to make free video and voice calls, send instant messages and share files with other Skype users. People also use Skype to make low-cost calls to landlines and mobiles.

For elegant simplicity, it's hard to go past Flickr:

> Share your photos. Watch the world.

4 Tell it in pieces. Pithy pieces. Because online readers scan, you need to think of copy differently for the web. Your website is no place for waffle, dense narrative recitals, banal generalities and abstraction. Readers want pithy summaries and compelling real-world examples.

5 Think hard about the five or six categories into which you can break up your business story—your tabs. And phrase them briefly but distinctively. Your categories ought to position you and your lines of work the way you want them understood, but they must also anticipate the needs and expectations of a reader. *Mark*, *Writing*, *Teaching*, *Consulting*, and *News* are the categories Mark came up with for his website (marktredinnick.com.au). His challenge was meeting the needs of readers, for some of whom he's a poet and essayist and for some a writing teacher and consultant.

The Australian Tax Office uses the categories *Individuals*, *Businesses*, *Non-Profit*, *Government*, *Tax Professionals* and *Super Funds*, which is probably about right, given the extent of their charter, although it presents something of a dilemma for a business person who's a sole proprietor. And it feels a bit too much like one of those speech recognition menus most organisations use these days to filter calls. Make sure you cater for the person who doesn't think of themselves in one of your categories; have a place they can go with a generic inquiry. But, more generally, have someone, metaphorically, to greet visitors at the door.

6 But sum it up first. Prowling the public and private sector websites of the world, we notice how few big institutions (government departments, telecommunications companies, banks, universities, big professional services firms) have engaging openers. There's no big picture; no front door. You click and encounter a mass of boxes, tabs, windows, drop-down menus. Greet them first. Show them a way in. Who you are and what you think you do, and how you define yourself are important matters to readers, especially on a first visit. So work on your opening page. In particular tell the big story, the story—briefly, of course—of who you are and what role you play in the world and why anyone would want or need to deal with you.

   But not like this.

> Here you will find information including current facts, figures, and historical data that allow you to learn more about the company from which you're renting a car or truck or equipment, or leasing a vehicle. Visit us often for informative updates!

7 Don't feel you have to say everything. You'd want your website to leave nothing material out, of course; it should give a reader a fast but thorough tour of your organisation and its soul—your skillsets, philosophies, key people, activities, triumphs and honours. But it doesn't have to—indeed, it shouldn't—answer every question about you they didn't know they had to ask. It should start a conversation, not stop it. So choose the pieces of your story that say most about you and what makes you distinctive. Tell those. Leave the detail for later.

   Lead prospective customers easily to the contact door you want them to find you by. You want something between ignored and swamped. Including the contact address, email address or phone number you want them to use on every web page is a good way to do this.

8 Make prices, dates, places, products and other such details easy to find. It's a visual medium, not a text-based medium. Use dot points and colour.

Academic Earth (www.academicearth.org) offers 'Free video courses from leading universities', featuring '20 new courses from Yale, Stanford and Harvard'. There are two simple menus, one listing participating universities, the other listing subjects, and there are stills from sample lectures as well as featured courses and lectures and top-rated courses and lectures.

6 Minutes

Minutes are so easy to write—badly. Which is a shame, since they matter so much.

Minutes provide a record of what key corporate meetings discuss and decide; they're written for posterity, for the markets, for other stakeholders, including the regulators, and to help the people who attended remember what they said and what they agreed to do. Minutes are a practice of good governance, and they are, if you want them to be, an operational tool—they can set tasks and define strategies for the weeks and years ahead. For these reasons, they ought to be the clearest, cleanest copy an organisation writes. They ought to be accurate and limpid and useful. Usually, they're not.

You're trying to record precisely who said what, and you're trying to do it objectively, and you're trying to do it accurately, and everyone's talking in tongues, and they're doing it fifteen to the dozen, not to mention the assorted nods, winks, whispered asides and body language that you never get to see while you're trying to take notes. You need ears in the back of your head. You need great shorthand, you need a perspicacious chair, and you need practice.

The particular convention that makes minutes so impenetrable is the habit of writing them in stiff sentence fragments written in the passive voice.

> It was noted that several applications had been received by the closing date. Following discussion, it was agreed that the position would be re-advertised with a view to attracting further expressions of interest.

It doesn't require a huge leap of imagination to suspect that a minute such as this conceals more than it reveals.

Of the key things to say about minutes, this is the most important: write them in the active voice.

'It was decided that a logo be designed' and 'Concerns were raised about the office relocation' and 'Statements of financial interest are to be submitted to the CFO' and 'It was decided that a new marketing strategy be developed and presented at the next meeting' tell us something, but not as much as they should, bearing in mind posterity and transparency and clarity. The passive voice—used in minutes partly as a way of affecting objectivity and partly because it's sometimes so hard to keep track of who says what—fails to tell management and the markets and anyone with a stake in the decision *who*; it doesn't attribute responsibility for the relevant action. And who's going to do these things, and who exactly raised the concerns, and who (the meeting, normally) exactly made the relevant decisions: these are matters of more than merely syntactical interest. To say *who* is to make things clear, and to support good governance and management.

- The meeting asked Dee Morgan to approach Deb Hooper to design the new logo.
- Juliet asked whether the relocation of company's headquarters and registered office to the Bahamas might be intended to secure certain tax benefits rather than to serve the mission of the company.
- All managers and staff must lodge statements of their financial interests with the CFO by 31 July.
- In response to the public outcry, the meeting asked Heather to

come up with a new marketing strategy for Vegemite and to present it at the next board meeting.

Good minutes keep it simple, but they name names. See what *The Little Red Writing Book* says about who-does-what sentences (chapter 2), and try to write those. In addition, then, to writing actively and favouring simple sentences that stay concrete and specific and refer to people and employ clear verbs of action,

- name the person responsible for each action decided upon
- if there's a task, put a due date on it
- if a number of views are expressed, if there's debate, try to summarise each, and who held it
- keep everything as trim as you can, but above all be very clear.

Meetings with any degree of formality will generally follow an agenda. If you're writing the minutes of a meeting with an agenda, use the agenda as your template. The meeting might not follow the agenda entirely, but some meetings do, and if they don't, that's something that really ought to be recorded, too. Was there a legitimate deferral of an item, did the meeting descend into chaos, did the chair fall asleep?

If you like, you can construe minutes minimally, as a notation of key decisions, performed mostly to comply with statutory requirements. On the other hand, you might choose to use the minutes as a management tool. In that case, the chair needs to make it clear that this is an agreed approach, and ensure that the minutes are written—and read—as guidelines to key actions.

By all means use dot points, but favour orthodox sentences. Minutes are not meant to be like jottings; they're pieces of writing, often crucial ones. And the unit that makes the fastest and fullest sense in writing is the sentence.

Write minutes not just to please the people who attended the meeting—your only duty to them is to write the truth; write so that the minutes might be clear five years down the track, to an interested outsider, or a court of law.

As a matter of procedure, some minute-takers circulate draft minutes to the people (or some of them) who attended the meeting. This is a good idea, but it can make it hard to settle on a final agreed form of words. The chair of the meeting is the person who needs to sign off on the minutes, so confer closely with her or him. But whatever else you do, write the minutes so they make good sense fast, and not only to the people who were at the meeting.

Good minutes include action points. For each item. Here's a tip: settle the action points first and circulate them as soon as possible following the meeting; don't wait till you've wrestled the minutes into shape and won final approval for them in all their glory. It's amazing how quickly things can be forgotten or remembered in a different light.

7 Media releases

Write a media release as though you were a journalist unassociated with your company. Practise detachment; step back from your habitual tropes, your corporate idiom; contemplate the organisational triumph, the mass sacking, the merger, the profit result, the conclusions of your audit, the results of your experiment, the sales numbers, the move of your manufacturing operations offshore ... from the point of view of a detached observer.

Write the story you want the press to run—word for word, if you can. But know that they won't (they shouldn't, and you shouldn't expect them to) run it in the way you might write about it in-house—triumphal, evasive, managerial, bureaucratic, academic, legalistic, or scientific; don't write it in the kind of prose the briefing documents you received were probably written in. They're not running your business or doing your bidding; they're informing and entertaining the public, which is their business. So they'll run your story, if they run it at all, in the sort of language stories need. And if you don't like the language (or the politics behind it) with which the press tell stories, write the story better. Look at it from their perspective; they're busy, deadlines are looming, they've got a page to fill, and a compelling, well-written story that's going to resonate with their readers suddenly lands, fully formed, on their desk. What's not to like? And a word of warning; stories in bureaubabble just don't play.

A press story is a lead followed by some vivid detail. A lead is what your thing amounts to in a sentence. Not some lofty abstraction, not the fact that your research breaks new ground—what new ground, how, why, when and where and for whom and why that matters. In a sentence. The rest of the story is whatever numbers, quotes, explanations, expert opinions, examples and illustrations you need to offer to ground, justify and flesh out the lead.

Here are some leads that work.

> Paying the lowest price for your website isn't always the most cost-effective way to reach your customers, according to experienced marketing specialist Jane Dear.
>
> A new guide, launched today by the Minister for Small Business Development, removes the guesswork from hiring freelancers.
>
> As reported recently in numerous media outlets, many companies are struggling with the implementation of environmentally friendly practices. Green Dreams is proud to offer a range of solutions for businesses of all shapes and sizes.
>
> Banks, the regulator and Storm Financial's founders are at a road block about who should be accountable for the failure of margin lending calls to reach margin loan borrowers.

And remember: if you're sitting on a lead, a thing you'd rather not, for whatever reason, say in so many words, you can be sure the press will—and you can be sure the way they report it won't be as pretty as you might make it. So say it your way and try to stop them spinning it in a way you may like less. We're talking PR 101 here, we know. Don't try to fool the press or the public, but by all means write the lead the way you think the story really runs. It's okay to manage the message, but even though they're sometimes lazy, like the rest of us, the media are not, on the whole, stupid.

Your purpose isn't to spruik or cover up or crow or blame or shame: it's to find and tell the story of the facts. A little detachment will help. And if you don't want the media to muck it up, or get it wrong, get it right and write it so well they stick to your script.

8 Newsletters

When you write a newsletter, you really do write the news. Only, the news, as with a website, is not the real point. The stories you tell, the information you offer, are a cover for the real enterprise, which is marketing—making connections, developing relationships, keeping yourself and your work in the market's mind. Newsletters are for branding; in particular, they're for building and maintaining community. They're for making and sustaining connection with one's constituencies. Businesses, public and private, use newsletters, delivered online or in the old-fashioned paper-based way, to stay in the hearts and minds of their customers and their employees—their external and internal stakeholders.

By spreading the word across your catchment about what you've done, what your people have succeeded at, what fun you've all had, what new products and ideas you've got to offer, how you've contributed to the welfare of the community, you're really advancing the story of who you are and, by implication, why you'd be good to form or sustain a relationship with.

The perfect newsletter understands this game but doesn't give it away. You write a good newsletter by writing it like the best kind of news bulletin your readers are likely to get. The more your copy sounds like selling, the less likely it is to sell anything.

Most of the best tips for pulling this off, we've already given you (see 'Website copy' and 'Media releases').

- Keep the items trim. A paragraph or two will usually do it. If you want to say more, provide a link or attach a file.
- Write a strong lead.
- Tell it like a story: avoid, in other words, anything like the idiom of the boardroom, the policy shop, or the market; write it in clear, vivid words that make sense fast to readers who'd rather be doing anything else.
- Focus on people, places, things, events. People like to read about people: stories inform and entertain by showing people doing things in the real world.
- Ration the passive voice. Cut it back hard.
- Talk the news items out in the voice you'd like your enterprise to have. Good stories speak in human voices.
- Let photographs and captions do most of the talking—and keep the captions singing.

These are, of course, the usual rules. Here are some other tips more specific to the business newsletter.

- Set up some regular columns or departments. Newsletter deadlines have a habit of coming round fast, and it's easier to meet them when you have a rough editorial template established. Readers like the continuity, too: it implies that you know what you're doing and have some design sense; it makes for faster and tidier reading; it establishes loyalty between them and the columns (and the columnists, if you name them, and if the columns have some personality).

- Don't make it all about you. Include some items that engage with relevant stories and developments in the political, cultural, legal and geographical environment in which you and your target readers work. And don't call it 'The Marketing Manager's Newsletter'. It's not yours; it's for everyone.
- Tell life stories. Always include an item on the lives of your employees, partners, board members and managers. Not just their successes, and not just their work lives. Remember: people like to read about people.
- Entertain them. By the quality, above all, of your storytelling and writing style (and design and illustration), but also by including light-hearted stories, cartoons and (if they're cool and tasteful) jokes.
- Help them. Give your readers tips on how to make the most of your products and services, how to fix them if they break, or upgrade them, if they want to; show them how you can help them respond to new challenges—legislative, technological, whatever. Case studies are a powerful way to spread the word on how your products and services can improve people's lives. Look nimble and up-to-date, and ready and able to help solve their problems.
- Invite them in. Newsletters are about community (and through it, of course, sales or PR). So ask readers to contribute stories or comments or ideas; run competitions; dedicate a column to readers' stories. This achieves more than extended mailing lists; it nurtures belonging and goodwill.
- Take the newsletter seriously. Recruit a good writer-editor-designer, and pay them well; value the task, don't just tack it on to someone's job description; skill your writer up. It's that old return on invest-

ment thing again.

Here's some good newsletter copy.

> Welcome to this month's newsletter. In this edition, we meet our new Chief Executive Officer Jane Smiley, discover what the team in IT have been cooking up to make your life easier, and conclude our three-part series on how to write more effectively at work.

Where newsletters are distributed electronically, as is so often the case these days, the same rules apply as for website copy. Perhaps a topical photo can be used up-front, highlighting a recent event or achievement, followed by an enticing list of contents.

9 Job applications and resumés

If an employer spends a minute-and-a-half looking over your resumé, consider yourself lucky. Job applications, on the whole, are about as much fun to read as they are to write. So make yours stand out fast—make it elegant, particular, brilliant even. Not crazy, unless you are, and you think they'll want that—just more than merely bland.

The purpose of the application and resumé—or whatever particular combination of documents the job ad asks for—is to get you an interview. It's to get you a ticket to the dance. With luck, you'll have the right moves from there.

Showing you can read and address a set of specifications will be a good start; using some of the key words they're looking for will be helpful, too. (Frighteningly, many employers now use search engines to scan applications for the key words they think distinguish the people they're looking for.) But so far, you're probably still back in the peloton. To get to the front, you need to take a risk; you need to show your colours. (Of course, they may not like your colours, but the sooner you both find that out, the better.) There's not much point in blending in; it's crowded back in the pack, and there can only be one winner. You need to find some language and a strategy that make you sound like you—a *you* who can do the job, for sure, but above all a distinctive, accomplished individual.

As with so much else, writing a job application is a positioning challenge. They want someone—but not just anyone; not just someone who sounds like everyone else and who managed to address the selection criteria—who can do the job, even bring new ideas and talents to the organisation, and who looks likely to be a fit. You want the job, or you wouldn't be applying; but you want them to recruit the real you, not a person they think you are.

So, here's the most important tip for writing job applications: don't conform. Cover the bases, of course, in a reasonably conventional manner, but don't write the same way, and say the same things, everyone else does. Playing it safe is the riskier course.

Tell the story of who you are, and why you fit the bill, and how, better than anyone, you'd thrive in the role.

Most private sector jobs want a cover letter and a resumé (*curriculum vitae*—CV, for short—is another name for the same thing); most public sector jobs want a statement addressing the selection criteria, plus a resumé. So, first some tips on resumés; then some on the statement on the selection criteria; then the cover letter.

RESUMÉ

Everyone knows roughly how a resumé goes, right?

Keep it to three or four pages, and structure it like this.

- Contact and personal details (including your age and marital status, if you like, but not if you think it won't help).
- A (short and compelling) summary of who you are and what you've achieved, and what you want to do with your working life from here;

where your strengths lie; the talents, skillsets, and personal qualities that set you apart.

- Your work experience, starting with a one-paragraph career overview, followed by a list of your employment history, starting with the most recent job. The entry for each job describes the employer's line of work, what you were responsible for in your role, and what you achieved. Briefly.

  At Fremantle Arts Centre Press, a small specialist publisher, I developed a list of picture books for young readers, which produced a 35% increase in sales revenue over two years.

- Your education and training, leading with your most advanced degree and working back to school graduation. List professional development, skills-based training and short courses separately.
- A list of your clients, if you've been self-employed.
- Professional memberships.
- Your interests, social and cultural activities, if you want.
- Referees.

Tips

- Although a lot of resumés are made of sentence fragments because the writer is shy of 'I', the first person is the neatest and most natural way to refer to yourself in a resumé, just as it is anywhere else. Another option is to write about yourself in the third person: 'Anna Swir is an award-winning copywriter and editor. She has worked freelance and for organisations in many parts of the world.' In dot points listing your responsibilities, you could drop 'I', but in general, avoid this kind of thing: 'managed a team of twenty-five reps', 'reporting to the managing director, responsible for the conception, design, build and operational delivery of ABC's IT system', 'have driven change programs related to organisational change'.

- Write sentences, even in your dot points. We live in times cursed by the tyranny of the dot point; tell a story, instead.
- Use dot points, by all means, but not too many, and certainly not exclusively. Applications made entirely of dot points will tell a truncated and generic story. Use them, instead, to break up your sentences and to highlight key achievements; you don't want to get too text-heavy.
- Avoid abstract, lofty, airy statements, even when you think they're hitting some of the requisite notes. How is something like this meant to distinguish you and make it sound like you have some clear and original thoughts in your head?

My mission is to utilise my skills in a professional environment for the mutual benefit of my employer and myself.

I am committed to adding value by applying my extensive knowledge, skills and experience to the challenges confronting the organisation.

The experience I have gained in a range of roles will enable me to leverage business opportunities in a proactive way.

- Write as concretely as you can, even in your summaries.

Reporting to the Managing Director, I ran the HR function; additionally I had responsibility for ISO implementation and accreditation. In this role, I also managed the phasing out of WordPerfect and the introduction of Novell.

Over the past three years, Ericsson UK has been through rapid business transformation, as the company has retrained and redeployed 2000 people from mobile operators H3G, T-Mobile, Vodafone and O2, acquired by Ericsson [or whatever]. Reporting to the Director of

Business Operations, I built and led a team that delivered organisational change management services on each of these transformation programs; my team provided thought leadership and established best practice approaches to complex IT transformations and global cultural change.

STATEMENT ADDRESSING THE SELECTION CRITERIA

Some jobs, especially in education and the public sector, ask you to write a statement explaining how you and your experience meet the selection criteria (often vague, sometimes quite specific) outlined in the duty statement. In addition, you may want to, or you may be asked to, submit your resumé. (In which case, take the chance to update it to address the nature and particulars of the job on offer.) But it's the statement addressing the selection criteria that will likely win or lose you the interview.

There's scope to be more discursive in your response than in the resumé and cover letter; and don't miss the opportunity to write in a manner that distinguishes you—a matter of writing, as ever, with grace, care and simplicity, while rationing the bureaucratese, including the language of the duty statement, you use in your responses. On the other hand, each of your responses must engage, from start to finish, with the particular criterion it concerns, making the case for how you fulfil it.

But be warned, as if you didn't know already: writing such statements can bring on a sudden and severe attack of boredom; just make sure your response does not, itself, induce sleep in its readers. The trick is to stay fiercely focused on the criteria without parroting the language they're phrased in. Think hard about what they want to hear, but sound like yourself in saying it.

It's often a good idea, before you start writing, to pick up the phone and talk with the contact person. It's uncanny how often the real job doesn't quite find its way into either the job description or the selection criteria. Talking to someone can give you some of the slender particulars, some of the texture, of the job itself and of the human environment in which it will be performed. A little conversation can reify a job—a thing that helps most people write an application with more confidence and voice. It's probably sensible to hop onto the organisation's website and get a handle, through its mission, values, philosophy and strategy statements, on what it's really about. You'll want your statement to demonstrate, in subtle ways, that you have such an understanding—and you're not likely to get it from the package they send you.

Start your response with a brief overview of your work life and personal strengths and how they recommend you for the position. Include your interpretation of what the position entails and demands and how and why you think you can perform it beautifully. Keep this to a paragraph—three sentences at most. But don't miss this chance to fly free of the criteria and sound a little like yourself.

> I should begin, as I encourage other writers of such documents to begin, with a deft summary. Here are some of the reasons you might think of for appointing me to this role.
>
> - I am the author of one of the leading guides for creative writers, *The Little Red Writing Book* and its companion *The Little Green Grammar Book*.
> - Those books arose out of nearly fifteen years of teaching creative and functional writing to a wide range of aspiring writers.
> - I am a poet and essayist and the author of six books, most recently *The Blue Plateau*, with two volumes of poetry forthcoming, two books under contract, and other essays, poems and books in the works.
> - I have a PhD in literature, a publishing track record as a literary critic, and experience teaching writing and mentoring writers at university level.
> - Before I started writing, I spent ten years as a book editor and publisher, which makes me, I guess, an industry insider, as well as a mature and productive writer and engaging writing teacher.

So, let me flesh that out a bit.

After that, make a heading of each criterion and respond to it, starting in each case with a sentence summarising your experience and training in the area alluded to by the criterion. Then include one or two instances from your work experience that support your case.

Something like this, though you should be able to muster a little more pizzazz:

> **Experience in staff supervision and training.** As a result of many years' experience in staff supervision, I have developed expertise in assessing the strengths of various members and supporting them to achieve their potential. [Follow with the examples.]

Structure your examples in the format of a short report, advises Deborah Barit, in an article in *The Australian*.

In other words, something like this.

> When I was appointed to lead the publishing team at NAO, I inherited a team of twenty-five staff, whom I had to lead through a process of adjustment to the outsourcing of the print function. This meant sourcing, designing and introducing training programs, guiding some staff through redundancy and recruiting new staff ... Employing mentoring and coaching techniques and leadership skills I studied in my Harvard MBA, and working with outsourcing and training consultants as required, I reduced staff numbers to fifteen over twelve months and increased the department's productivity by 50 per cent—halving its costs and doubling the speed of production of reports against the levels of the previous year.

Close your response by asserting, quietly, that your experience meets the criterion and will allow you to perform this aspect of the job.

Deborah Barit advises writing your response to each criterion as a separate piece of writing. This will help you bring freshness to each entry; it's an antidote to repetitiveness—a good thing to ration, but impossible to avoid completely, since most duty statements include overlapping categories. Although there's some scope for cross-referencing another answer, you should try to make each section stand alone.

When you think you're finished, stand back. You're probably not there yet. Let a little time pass, if there's any left to leave. Reread all your responses and edit out undue repetition in your language and content. Edit the whole thing carefully, and more than once, to make it trim and lean, and to weed out typos, grammar gaffes and awkwardness.

Tips

- How long is a good statement? Five pages would be a good upper limit. But the length of your whole statement and each section within it will depend on how many criteria there are and how much experience you have to talk about. There's no perfect length. But you want it to feel trim. Place a limit of three paragraphs on each response, and see how that works. Take another if you need it. Just make sure that if you add length, you add value.
- Focus on the criterion from the very first sentence; don't just open your mouth and start talking around the point. We've said this above, but it bears repeating. Start with a summary sentence; follow with an example or two; use a structure for spelling out those examples; close with a summary that makes the case for how your examples demonstrate your fulfilment of the criterion in question.
- Rather than repeat abstract and unfocused language from a criterion, and to make sure you say something meaningful yourself, start by saying what it means to you in the context of the department's mission and the job description.
- Avoid or find variations for 'In this role I had responsibility for' and 'extensive experience'. Try instead, 'I headed', 'I managed' or even simply 'I was responsible for', and 'I have worked in this field for ten

years' or 'The decade I have spent'.

- Vary your language, about similar things, generally: 'I managed the implementation …'; 'I put in place …'; 'I oversaw the …'; 'Under my management …'; 'My staff were successful in …'; 'My most significant achievement …'

COVER LETTER

Keep your cover letter to a page, if you can, and use it to highlight why you'd be the best person for the job.

Start with something catchy, but not too cheesy. This is a snazzy beginning to a cover letter to the publishers HarperCollins (who published the book the applicant refers to in her opening).

> Like Henry the bookeating boy, I love books; like him, I no longer devour them. Which makes me the perfect candidate for the position of distribution centre manager you advertised in the *Moss Vale Times* last weekend. I have, in addition, ten years' experience as a bookseller and ten further years as the mother of book-devouring boys, one of them in fact named Henry.

Allude to discussions you've had about the job, if you've had them, or comment on why you came to apply—particularly if someone of note suggested it. Try not to sound too desperate, on the one hand, or pompous, on the other. Write with confidence (see 'Assertiveness 101' in chapter 2). Refer to your resumé, but try not to repeat too much of it.

Here's a whole cover letter that came our way recently.

> After talking with you the other day at the suggestion of Professor Beckett, I'm delighted to apply for this position, which I'd be interested in taking on fulltime.
>
> As my resumé outlines, I've taught (through ANU's extension program mostly) and written for journals and newspapers in financial planning

for a dozen years and more, after a decade as an accountant with PWC, and a brief time as a lawyer before that. I'm also the author of a couple of key books on auditing and performance management, *The Audit Book* and *The Performing Flea*. A few years ago I wrote a doctoral dissertation praised for its lucidness of expression and its academic rigour—soon after published, with little change, as a book (*The Performing Flea*).

Though I move happily in accounting, business and government environments, universities, as I may have said when we spoke, are my native habitat. I look forward to the chance to work in one, especially the one at which I gained my MBA.

I look forward to talking with you and your colleagues very soon about the position.

10 Proposals

The proposal is a business staple. Most of us get more chances to write them than we'd probably like. On the one hand, they're such an inclusive category, it's hard to say much of relevance to every proposal writer. On the other hand, the idea is always much the same, so there are lessons everyone can apply in any situation.

Whenever one writes, especially in business and the wider fields of organisational and professional prose, one is trying to persuade. You have a thought, a product, a service, a diagnosis, some advice, a thesis ... and you'd like the reader to share it; you have a story, and you'd like them to join it. But the proposal is out and out persuasion; its function is to put a proposition, and with luck close the deal on it.

Proposals are either solicited or unsolicited.

Solicited proposals (of which a job application is one variety) respond to invitations—to express interest, to apply for a gig or to bid for some project. Someone lets a tender or publishes an invitation for proposals (sometimes called a request for proposal, or RFP)—to run a course, to build an Olympic stadium, to fix the train system, to develop a site, to join a business or educational partnership—your response will be a solicited proposal. Like a job application, the aim of your response to an RFP is to stand out among dozens or hundreds of others—to get on the short list and have a shot at the prize. Much of what we say below applies to writing solicited proposals, too, but in these instances, you'll normally have to fit your response to a template of some kind; or, like a job application, again, speak to prescribed criteria. What we had to say about all that above applies here, too.

Unsolicited proposals are your own idea, but it should be said, the two categories are not discrete. Sometimes you write a proposal after forming a relationship with a prospective client, customer or partner, and in response to an informal invitation; or you make a proposal to an existing client for upgrading the IT system you installed for them two years ago. But in these cases, as with unsolicited proposals you write cold, you have total control over the shaping of the document.

So, solicited or unsolicited, or somewhere in between, you might write a proposal

- to get an arts or industry grant or fellowship
- to get a loan
- to float a company
- to sell a book idea to a publisher, a story to a journal, a film script or concept to an agent
- to invite a benefactor to support your festival or event
- to sell a financial product to a new client
- to convince a vendor to sell her home through you
- to change policy in your organisation, or across the jurisdiction
- to suggest to your board a new way of doing business

- to pitch a new workshop to a training provider
- to have your client buy the new system

and to pursue a thousand other bright ideas.

But the idea is always the same. You have a *case*; your proposal *puts it*—upfront, briefly and very clearly, if it's a useful kind of a proposal. Then the proposal, by various means, *makes it*—it sells the proposition.

One way or another, the proposition is either *you have a need that I can meet (better than anyone else)* or *I have a need that you can meet* or, in the case of changes to national law and policy, *we all have a need that this proposal meets*.

You identify a need (yours or theirs), and you propose a solution.

To write a winning proposal, then, you'll want to get smart about these three things:

- having a case (a matter of inspiration and clear thinking)
- putting a case (a matter of clear, trim expression)
- making a case (a matter of rhetoric).

Having a case is a matter of working out what, precisely, you are putting forward. You get there by thinking long and hard and straight. Your case is what is often called the *thesis*, or the *lead*. See what we've said in chapters 2 and 3 (specifically, the twelve big ideas and the virtues of flow and finish) and what we add in chapter 5. See what Mark has to say about what a thesis is, and how you get one, in chapter 6 of *The Little Red Writing Book*. The answer is SEX (State, Explain, eXplore) and a good mindmap. Your thesis, your proposition, is the point your whole document reaches—what it amounts to. It is the thing you state, then explain and explore. Just don't think you're ready to write your proposal until you've worked out exactly what you're proposing.

Putting a case is writing your thesis—putting your case on paper. It's your elevator pitch—your thing, in thirty seconds. It will happen easily if you've done your thinking well and if you observe most of the heavenly virtues of writing well.

- Start with your proposition; make it the very first thing you write. Not *This document proposes a solution*, but *I propose that we form a partnership to acquire the old Maltings building in Burrawang and develop the site over the next five years as a centre for arts and arts industries*. A client of Mark's, who chaired meetings of a policy proposals committee, used to complain that, notwithstanding a form that insisted that writers state their proposal upfront, most writers managed to make him start reading the proposal at the end to work out what it wanted him to focus his mind on from the start. Don't make your reader start at the end. Make it easy. Put your case in the opening paragraph.
- Spend at most two or three sentences on it. Contextualise it a bit; state the problem and the answer; summarise quickly why you're the one for them, and allude to the demonstrations and examples you'll supply in the body of the proposal.
- Make it clear, trim and vivid. Don't oversell here—or in the rest of the proposal, for that matter. The most compelling case is the most adroitly worded—deft, confident, plain. Strive to communicate, not to impress, as June Campbell puts it.

Making the case is most of the document. It's where you convince your reader of the case you put so elegantly at the start. No matter how compellingly put, a proposition without a justification is just an assertion. You make a case by

- using persuasive language
- describing clearly the scenario you engage with, your skills or needs, your people, the environment and so on (This is the rhetorical mode known as *description*)

- explaining your approach or the system you want to employ, or how your book will work—making anything technical, in other words, transparent to a reader in a hurry (*Exposition*)
- deploying well-chosen case studies, graphics, illustrations, examples and testimonials to speak to your skills and successes (*Narration*)
- arguing for the solution you propose (their money, your services, your policy amendment) to the issue as you define it, using logic, reference to authoritative literature, allusion to first principles like efficiency, public good, shareholder value, morale, environmental sustainability, the advancement of wisdom … and whatever other rhetorical devices you can think of. Without, again, overdoing it (*Argumentation*).

Beyond this, all the usual writing rules apply.

- In particular, ration your technical jargon. You have to put the case in language your reader—think of her as an intelligent non-expert in a hurry—is likely to make sense of fast. Don't use technical language unless it helps; offer easy translations if you can't avoid the technicality.
- Worse than technical jargon is false elegance. Don't waffle. Keep it trim; speak it like you mean it.
- Errors of all kinds look bad in a proposal, especially if it is nicely turned out. Typos and grammar glitches scream 'careless' and 'unprofessional'. Watch your step. Employ an editor; pay them well.
- Make it look great. Cool but readable typeface; cool but readable page design. Colour, but not too much. Graphs and illustrations, but not too many. Often, these days, you'll deliver it electronically *and* in hard copy. If there's a hard-copy edition, choose a smart stock (not too white, not too thin); bind it smartly, too.
- Emphasise the benefits your proposal will bring—to you, to them, to

the organisation, to the law, to the world.

- Make the cost or price easy to find and understand.
- Use headings and subheadings to make your logic—the proposal's narrative line—easy to see and to follow.

There's no one right way to structure a proposal. Sometimes you have to follow a template. So follow it—that's one less thing to worry about. But under each heading apply all these tips and all the first principles. Start everything with its main point.

Proposals differ widely in the culture and expectations that surround them. But here's a rough structure to adapt.

- Executive summary
- What we propose (your introduction, including your elevator pitch)
- Our analysis of your need/what we need (this won't always be necessary)
- Who we are and what we do
- Our people
- Our experience (including examples and case studies of analogous work; lists of clients and projects)
- What our clients say about us (testimonials, references, reviews)
- Our solution in detail
- How it will help (benefits section, focused on, but not limited to, their needs, or yours)
- What it will cost
- Cost–benefit analysis and conclusion
- What next (point the way ahead: what you want them to do next;

what you will do next).

We're not suggesting these as your headings, although you could do a lot worse. These are ways of saying very plainly what each section of your report addresses.

11 Instructional writing

We have in mind here manuals and other documents written to explain—and help others (staff and customers) perform—technical processes and procedures:

- safety manuals
- recipes
- guidelines to help staff and customers lodge applications (for leave, for funding, for exemption) and offer feedback
- manuals to help customers assemble or install (and initialise) products (barbecues, home entertainment systems, credit cards)
- routine procedures (performing a backup of the organisation's computer system, recording the monthly photocopier usage)
- certified agreements (terms and conditions applying to the workplace).

Although—because, really—it's the most functional of all functional writing, instructional copy needs to imagine and address its readers' needs better than any other. Strange though it may sound, good instructional writing is empathy embodied. You've got to enter into it like a conversation. You're telling people what to do; most likely they won't or can't do it without instruction—so they're depending on you. And you're not there to show them or do it for them. You need to anticipate their next move and guide them before they make it; see their next question coming and answer it first. Like all organisational writing, but more so, you're making something that's complex clear. Right now.

All this you must deliver without dropping the technical ball.

And because good instructional writing can be the difference between safety and injury (life and death, even), product satisfaction and consumer rage, staff engagement and organisational malaise, you'll need to take as much care with it as you ever take at a keyboard: the care to ensure your words mean absolutely and only what you intend them to mean; that you speak specifically and concretely.

Finally, too, you're going to have to be very logical and sequential. You can't afford to miss a step.

This writing matters so much that you might think of hiring a technical writer. Technical writers have mastered the acts of imagination, the feats of exposition and the clarity of diction you're going to need.

If you want or need to do it yourself, here are some tips.

- Translate every technical expression. A glossary can help, but try to write so plainly that your reader doesn't need to find it.
- The imperative mood is made for instruction: *Find our web page, click 'registration' and follow the links*; *connect part A to part B*. Favour it over the clumsy old passive voice: *part A needs to be connected to part B*. Or 'should' usages: *applicants should follow the links on our website*; or the killer combination of both—*applications should be lodged in our offices by hand by 31 January*. (For more on the imperative mood and its uses, see *The Little Green Grammar Book*.)
- Walk yourself through the steps and write down what you do.
- Once you've written each draft, ask someone less expert than you to follow it (unless these are safety instructions, and imperfect prose may be a death sentence). If it's a recipe, ask them to try to cook the dish with no guidance from you or anyone else. Keep working until

your test user stops tripping over, asking questions, and complaining. Until it works—keeps them safe, gets the dish cooked.

- Avoid *must*, *should* and *shall* generally. (A client of Mark's once insisted on a difference between the connotation of *should* and *shall*, and relied on it in their safety instructions. And we're talking electricity generation here. Reliance on such a linguistic subtlety, he tried to advise them subtly, may not be a great way to manage the relevant risk, especially where the stakes are high.)
- Imagine your writing, instead, as your voice talking to them, leading them through. The imperative mood will be how that goes best. To get this right, talk your writing onto the paper; never stop talking it. This really is talk tidied.
- Numbered or dot points are a good idea. Headings, like *Step One*, *Step Two* do the trick, too. Avoid blocks of text.
- Check that everyone is using the same machine, system or version, and if they're not, make sure you provide alternative instructions as required.
- If things change, as things so often do, make sure the updated instructions are flawless—not half-baked, done on the fly, or disseminated by that old office favourite, Chinese whispers. Announce the changes in your newsletter, summarise them clearly, highlighting the important bits and their ramifications, and issue copies of the new instructions to everyone who needs them.

12 Speeches

If writing is talking on paper, making a speech may be writing out loud.

Which is to say, when you give a speech, as opposed to when you sit and write, you really are talking, and there really is an audience, and you'd better talk to them; but, if it's going to count, as some speeches are meant to, and if you want to keep your audience awake and engaged, you'd better take the kind of care with the script that a writer takes with every document that counts. If good writing is always talk tidied, a good speech is even more like talk and even tidier than ever.

Since one of the measures of good writing is how well it goes when you say it out loud—how pleasing its rhythm, how trim, how vivid, how clear its phrasing—learning to write well should help you write a good speech: this time you (or someone else) really will be saying it out loud, so you'd better make even surer than ever it talks. Take the care you'd always take; be personable, not formal, and certainly not pompous; observe the seven heavenly virtues and all the rest of it. But above all, work at your word choice, at the rhythms of your syntax and the shaping of your paragraphs, to have them sound like human utterance. Reading something out to a live audience will only work if it was written to be heard. For speeches are performed out loud between real people in real time; someone, an actual person, opens their mouth and the writing comes out. Speeches work best when their rhythms hold close to the rhythms, not of organisational cant, but of real human speech—and in particular the rhythms of the person speaking them.

A speechwriter, though, is not just *allowed* to scale back conventional phrasing and write with their ear (and tongue); it's compulsory. Bum notes, corporate claptrap and stiff formality, circumlocutions, evasions and bureaucratic clichés you can (almost) get away with on paper will clang in a speech.

A speech is slightly elevated talk: it should sound even more like actual talk than any other kind of writing, but it should also be worked a little harder than most writing, for elegance and grace. The formality that attends the making of a speech is best catered for not by means of etiquette but by way of eloquence and art; avoid too much 'it gives me great pleasure to' and 'unaccustomed as I am', favouring instead some shapely vernacular rhetoric.

This passage from Barack Obama's inaugural in 2009 illustrates all this. It may not be the finest inaugural address ever coined, but it's a strong speech. Though an inaugural is not the place for much policy detail, for instance, this passage, elegantly phrased, simply worded and rhythmic, nonetheless lays out an agenda the president can be held accountable for.

> That we are in the midst of crisis is now well understood. Our nation is at war against a far-reaching network of violence and hatred. Our economy is badly weakened, a consequence of greed and irresponsibility on the part of some but also our collective failure to make hard choices and prepare the nation for a new age.
>
> Homes have been lost, jobs shed, businesses shuttered. Our health care is too costly, our schools fail too many, and each day brings further evidence that the ways we use energy strengthen our adversaries and threaten our planet.
>
> These are the indicators of crisis, subject to data and statistics. Less measurable, but no less profound, is a sapping of confidence across our land; a nagging fear that America's decline is inevitable, that the next generation must lower its sights.
>
> Today I say to you that the challenges we face are real; they are serious and they are many. They will not be met easily or in a short span of time. But know this America: They will be met.

The agenda? Security, economic recovery, jobs growth, health, climate change.

How far, by comparison, is this kind of writing (we don't mean the subject matter, for anything is speech-worthy; we mean the words it uses and the way it strings them together) from belonging in a speech:

> Recording and analysing outcomes of active compliance and other deterrent activities are important to inform future planning and targeting of SNC compliance risk.

If you have to write speeches, read and listen to some great ones. Learn what you can about rhetoric and oratory. Practise the things we've said here. And when you're writing, keep sounding the speech out; say it to the mirror or to someone you love. Does it work when you say it? If, or where, it doesn't, change it so it does.

Beyond these practices and principles, though, here are some other quick tips.

1. Have a point; make it clearly; make it, mostly, at the start. 'There are only two things you need to master to write like a champion: choosing the right words, and putting them in the right order.' 'A conservative party without a policy on climate change is a party without a future.' 'Tonight let me outline the three changes we need to take to ensure the organisation's future.'
2. Give them one memorable line to take home—a line in which the personality and key message(s) of the speech are lodged: 'I have a dream …', 'Ask not what your country can do for you …', 'Judith Beveridge, in her poems, apprentices herself to what she does not know; she teaches us who we are by writing about who she isn't.' This could be your opening line or your close, or both, or something from in between.
3. If the speech is longish, explain its structure at the start and use headings or numbers to indicate each part.
4. Start with something personal (an anecdote, a joke, an aside, a quote), but don't go on too long about it. It helps to build rapport with your audience. Get to your point fairly fast and lay it out plainly.
5. If you don't want to spell out your main point(s) upfront, as President Obama didn't in his inaugural, make it (them) easy to find as the speech goes on. It would have been easy enough for Obama's listeners to pick out that policy agenda, which was the purpose—as well as giving hope and encouraging grit—of the speech, to give a commitment to.

6. Use the first person throughout, wherever it's appropriate. Someone, after all, is doing the talking here. It's nice to acknowledge her presence. But better than the first person, diction and syntax that belong in good speaking will keep the speech personable.
7. Tell stories. And don't call them 'case studies'. Just tell them. Nearly everyone loves to hear a story well told. Story makes even interest rates real.
8. Quote others—make sure the phrases you choose are at least as well made as your own, and that they support your point. *Ethics at Work* uses a quote (from literature, pop songs, film, the classics) to underline each of its values. One of them is this smart aphorism from Mark Twain: 'Always do right. This will gratify some people and astonish the rest.'
9. Project some images—not just graphs and charts. Make them relevant, of course, but also good to look at. Not so good, though, that you lose the attention of your audience. The event of the speech takes place in the words the speaker shares with the crowd; you need to hold their attention. A priest we know illustrates his homilies with images of saints, book covers, sacred sites and song lyrics; using a remote he points at his laptop from wherever he has wandered in the church.
10. Use PowerPoint, or something like it, sparingly, if at all. It can be helpful to articulate key messages and phrases and, for instance, a summary of the structure of the speech, visually. Don't put your whole speech up there, and avoid anything too wordy. If you can do without it, do without it. It isn't compulsory: speakers have survived for thousands of years without it. You want the audience looking at and listening to you; everything else is just decoration, at best, and at worst, distraction.
11. Repeat important messages. One approach is to start with them and close with them and separate each of them out and talk about it in the

body of the speech. Deft repetition helps listeners follow.

12 Use as little jargon as you can; if you use any, explain it gracefully.

13 Get technical, but not too technical. They'll understand numbers, but they may not follow an equation.

14 Close strongly, repeating the main idea(s), posing a challenge, pointing the way ahead, or quoting someone clever.

Many people, of course, have to write speeches to be delivered by someone else—their boss, the minister, the chairperson, the president. Where this is the case, everything we've said still applies. But the challenge has an extra dimension: you have to coin some words that sound natural coming out of someone else's mouth. You have to make them sound like themselves at their best. So, listen to them talking; tape them, and play the tapes back, and note their (best) characteristic turns of phrase, the strategies they favour for making points and building sentences. And write *with* them, if you can. Many of the best speechmakers have worked closely with their speechwriters: Paul Keating worked closely with Don Watson, for instance, and Bill Clinton with his writers. The speeches of those politicians were collaborative acts. Barack Obama, a trained and talented orator, writes many of his speeches himself, but he also uses a team of writers and works closely with them through many drafts to compose speeches.

Getting that close to the speechmaker, let alone working with them on the composition, isn't always possible. Do your best. Try to sit down with them at least once and listen to the way they put things. Get close enough often enough to work out what they want to say (get some dot points on key messages) and how they want to say it. Get some personal details from them; get them to tell you a story that bears on the theme; listen to how they speak.

We've written here about speeches, which are instances of writing. A presentation is another matter—an instance of communication but not of writing. You shouldn't *read* a presentation; you should talk it out, supported by good notes, PowerPoints and other peripherals. So we'll leave presentations, which are more about performance than about writing, to others to discuss.

CHAPTER 5

THE HELP DESK

Welcome to the help desk.

If you've come this far, you'll have your seven heavenly virtues down, and you'll have workshopped them on some key business documents. If you're starting here, you should note that the last chapter took apart twelve of the most common business documents, and showed readers how to put them back together again more elegantly. This is a trouble-shooting chapter; it offers guidance—*dos* and *don'ts*, tips and tricks—for handling many of the micro problems you'll encounter writing at work. It should help you find your way out of some of the tightest spots in business writing; it should help you write some seriously readable working sentences.

1 A few dot points on dot points

It's easy to make dot points; it's hard to make them well. Dot points are not meant to save writers the trouble of writing sentences; they're meant to help readers find key points fast. They're a visual device the purpose of which is to put some space around a few key and closely related points. Clutter kills them. So does bad grammar in and around them. So write sentences, and use dot points to display their key parts.

Dot points work well when

- each dot is a short phrase or clause (like this)
- each one runs no longer than this (try to keep each point from running over a line, like this)
- you don't use more than four or five
- you drop commas and semicolons between lines
- you end the last one with a stop.

For chapter and verse on dot-point etiquette, especially why the semicolon between items clutters a dot-point list and queers the elegance on which the device depends, see *The Little Green Grammar Book*. But in essence: although it's best to write dot points as parts of sentences, the layout makes the punctuation redundant. The line of space, the indent and the dot serve the purpose the punctuation does if you lay the sentence out the old-fashioned way—they keep the pieces apart. And since you were using dots to make things clear, don't muddy the picture again with dangling punctuation.

Decide whether your dot points are pieces of a sentence, disarticulated and laid out neatly, as above—or whether each dot point is itself a sentence—or even several sentences. We've used dot points this way through the last section of this book; it's a device, like numbering, that reminds a reader that what they're reading belongs in a list; the structure of your thinking is laid out.

But different rules apply when each dot point is a sentence or a paragraph—when, in other words, it stands on its own grammatically. Here are the rules.

- Because each item is a sentence (at least), use an initial capital on its opening word.
- Close each point with a full stop (not a semicolon).

- Introduce your list with a sentence (or more) and don't end that sentence with a colon. Introductory words that end in a colon begin a sentence, strictly speaking, that runs to the end of your last dot point.
- Don't let your dot-point list run for page after page. Consider numbers or, better still, subheadings, instead. A reader will get lost in a long sequence of dots.
- Think about using numbers instead if you're likely to refer back to the items. *As mentioned in the fourth dot point above* is a clumsy usage.
- And remember: dot points of the paragraph kind don't play well to an audience gazing at a screen in a darkened room. PowerPoint loves dot points that really are dot points. Paragraphs stacked and flagged with dots work nicely enough in expository writing on paper (and at a stretch on a website); PowerPoint presentations fail if you ask your audience to read sentences instead of listening to the ones coming out of your mouth.

This article in a medical journal uses dot points—each a paragraph made of one or more sentences—to highlight the main findings of a study.

> Study Highlights
>
> - Researchers examined the Spanish cohort of EPIC. They focused on 15,630 men and 25,808 women between the ages of 29 and 69 years.
> - Participants underwent a baseline assessment for dietary patterns and alcohol use. In addition, they were assessed for cardiovascular risk factors.
> - Men were divided into 6 categories based on their use of alcohol: former drinkers, never drinkers, low intake (0–5 g/day), moderate intake (5–30 g/day), high intake (30–90 g/day), and very high intake (> 90 g/day).
> - Women were categorized as former drinkers, never

drinkers, low intake (0–5 g/day), moderate intake (5–30 g/day), and high intake (30–90 g/day).

- The cardioprotective effect of alcohol consumption was statistically significant among men, but there were too few CHD events among women to demonstrate an independent protective effect of alcohol consumption.

Ethics at Work employs dot points elegantly, too.

Examples of unfair behaviour

- Playing dirty tricks or telling lies about your competitors in a new business pitch is unethical.

- Misrepresenting your agency's capability, expertise or billings to a potential client is unethical.

- Putting forward ideas that can't be achieved on budget, to win the business, is unethical.

And finally, use dot points sparingly. Too many can kill your message, if not the messenger. Or the audience. Dot points truncate; good writing flows. As the pet-shop owner says in Dr Seuss's story to the little boy about the fish food: so much, and no more.

2 A story tells a thousand pictures

If it's a piece of writing you're putting together, then most of it ought to be writing. Don't think for a moment that your graphics—your tables and charts, your maps and graphs, your equations and photos and logos—will get you off the textual hook. Don't let them stand in for what they're meant merely to illustrate, or depict differently or summarise—which is to say, whatever point it is you're trying to make, whatever story you're trying to tell.

You're talking here. On paper. And that goes best in words. Pictures help, of course. They give your reader a break; they reinforce a message; they speak especially to those whose intelligence runs more to images and numbers than words. But the words must carry the message; the graphics are just there to help.

So what you want is an integrated package: you introduce your point; you use a figure to illustrate that point vividly, having introduced the graphic element briefly; you draw out the meanings embodied in your picture. Talk about your graphs and Venn diagrams and tables and spreadsheets—they cannot speak for themselves. Some of us would rather hear about it, or else we don't respond quickly or deeply to numbers and tables and other non-verbal representations of the truth. But it's not really for that reason you need to spell your pictures out; it's because you're writing, here, and that means you're talking. So tell your reader what your fine pictures mean.

A picture is only as useful as the text around it is clear. Deft use of illustrations, though, and careful integration of complementary words and images make for elegant writing, and for smooth and pleasant reading.

Avoid tired, passively voiced references to graphics: *As demonstrated in Figure 1*, or *Our findings are represented in Table A*. Try, instead: *Figure 1 shows* or *The trend line in Figure 1 shows how*; *Consumer demand has far outstripped business confidence (Figure 2)*, or *Figure 20 summarises the state of current scientific knowledge.*

Explanatory captions help a reader read your charts, too: *Variation in the Earth's surface temperature, 1890–1990*; *Taxation expenditure as a percentage of total taxation receipts*; or something with a little more attitude, after the style of Alan Kohler on the ABC TV news—*Let's call the whole thing off*; *Ain't no cure*; *Hire power.*

And don't overdo the visuals. A few lines go a long way. If you turn your document into a slide show interrupted now and then by sentence fragments, you may invite suspicion that you're hiding the fact that you haven't really got all that much to say. Or the confidence to say it.

3 Heading in the right direction

Headings are short stories—*very* short stories. Flash non-fictions. The story each tells—obviously, in outline—is what the reader is about to learn. The better the heading is, the more it discloses, not just about the field that the next bit of copy covers—*Methodology*; *Findings*; *Conclusion*; *Organisational structure*; *Governance*; *Recommendations*—but what the words end up telling us.

Think how newspaper headlines, in their peculiar compressed syntax, summarise the story they head: *Charter plan in disarray*; *Obama awarded Nobel Prize*; *Ultimo gets the architect it deserves*; *Garnaut cool on stimulus*; *Standoff as hope for rivers runs dry*; *Treasury, Reserve split on outlook*; *Murdoch urges Beijing to stamp out intellectual piracy*; *Star struck by sexual harassment allegations*.

Headings help business prose. They advertise the structure of your story; they signpost the journey (often long and dry) the reader is taking through your words. They help you, the writer, stay somewhere near the track of your thinking, too. Don't be afraid to use them wherever, and as often as, they help: letters, web copy, proposals, reports, job applications. And make them as clear, specific and even vivid—and therefore as useful—as you like.

Nothing but convention compels you to use headings as plain and general as *Introduction*, *Background*, *Audit scope*, *Overall conclusion*, *Findings*, and so on. Instead of *Methodology,* you could use *Measuring consumer satisfaction by surveys*; instead of *Audit scope*, try *The audit focused on corporate governance*, or at least *What the audit covers*.

Earlier we listed many of the subheadings from the Stern Review, and commented how those subheadings, each a short story, add up to a telling, in brief, of the whole report; subheadings such as *The transition to a low-carbon economy will bring challenges for competitiveness but also opportunities for growth*.

In chapter 4 we noted the power and usefulness of some headings we found in a government audit, headings that make a technical and dryly analytical document much easier to navigate and even comprehend because of their narrative quality and specificity—headings like *MAL is a central element in border protection* and *PRIVACY: what agencies are required to do*. A small guide to climate change, from which we have also quoted already, uses these plainspeaking chapter headings (many of them questions): *What is global warming?*; *A brief history of the global warming hypothesis*; *Your viewpoint determines the future*; *What is the evidence for climate change?*; *How do you model the future?*; *What are the possible future impacts of global warming?*; *Surprises*; *Politics*; *What are the alternatives?*. These characterise the content of the parts of the whole and pull a reader in. The chapters of the same book employ subheadings of a similar, mind-focusing and concrete kind: *Storms and floods*; *What do the sceptics say?*; *Adaptation and mitigation*; *Future global temperatures and sea level*.

Questions can work well as headings: they address the reader; they anticipate the questions he or she might have and put them. Make sure you answer the questions your headings ask, though; more generally, deliver what your headings promise. Otherwise, you erode trust in the document. Clear statements (phrases or clauses, and ideally not too long) work just as well. Perhaps better—where they answer a question, rather than just asking it, they serve as a summary telling of the copy that follows. Headings that set up a list are powerful, too: *Twelve big ideas*; *Seven deadly sins*; *Ten ways to make a profit from your prose*; *Three ways to avoid a global depression*; *A five-step plan to keep the world from drowning*.

Such devices, employing a speaking voice, some clear thinking and a bit of verve, make a profound difference to a piece of functional writing. A reader can discern the issues and conclusions, and a fair bit of context, without being forced to discover it—sometimes buried quite deep—in the text. This approach to headings (and the thinking they articulate) doesn't just help the reader, though: it forces the writer to focus less on the detail and more on the overall storyline of the report they're writing—on what is material to the central question. The kind of clarity of thought and diction it models is likely to spill over into the sentences in the body of the report itself.

In one report Mark wrote recently, assessing the writing of a government agency, he used headings like these:

- Half as long—twice as good [this was the title of the report]
- The art of summary
- How to improve your report writing
- What you'll gain (what we'll all gain) if you write better summaries
- Why we conducted this review, which reports we reviewed, and how.

As in so many other areas of business writing, playing it safe—shying from such headings and subheadings—may succeed only in glazing the eyes of your readers.

4 Corporate clichés and how to live without them

A CLUTCH OF CORPORATE CLICHÉS

Here's a quick and dirty laundry list of some common corporate clichés. Using them isn't always sinful—it's possible we've used some in this book—but it's rarely a virtue. Use one now and then, if you can't do any better, but don't make a habit of it; never put one in a sentence without asking why you can't be plainer, shorter, clearer, more specific or more honest. There are, for instance, alternatives. All you have to do is ask yourself what you're really trying to say. (See the 'Good word guide' later in this chapter for a few suggestions.)

When we thought about it, there seemed to be several species of cliché, and this is how we've ordered our list; but clearly our categories overlap, for many of these words and phrases fit just as easily under more than one heading.

How many of these do you use?

Bureaucratic tics

Characterised by a tendency to favour three or more words where one might suffice, and to avoid the personal and particular, and to strike a sophisticated-sounding, not to say self-important, tone.

as discussed
going forward (why not 'over the coming year/five years' or 'in the years ahead'?)
further to
in relation to
with reference to
in respect of
with regards to
should you have any further queries please do not hesitate to contact
implement
at this point in time
at your earliest convenience
upon completion of the form
expedite
prior to
subsequently/subsequent to
consequently/consequent upon
in terms of
on a case-by-case basis
on a regular basis
documentation
allocate
instigate an inquiry
ascertain
execute
facilitate
perusal
feedback

Managerial idiom

Using polysyllabic, generalised, abstract, vaguely scientific- or technical-sounding words and phrases for things that could be and should be more plainly put (or sometimes where you're talking about nothing at all).

align
key (as an adjective with nouns like 'factors', indicators', 'players', 'deliverables', 'outcomes', 'success factors', and so on; or as in 'these factors are key')
deliverables
drivers
operationalise
initiative
future initiatives
new initiatives (if it's an initiative, it's new)
capability
competency
is responsible for/has responsibility for
framework
resource (as a singular, one-size-fits-all noun covering funds, services or possibly non-existent desirables; and as a verb)
drivers (of change, initiatives, a program, a program of change and/or initiatives; anything that hasn't got an engine and a steering wheel, really)
client (for people like refugees, prisoners, patients and others who have no choice in the matter)
value-adding/value-add (as a noun)/value-added (as an adjective)
effective and efficient
documentation
scope (as a verb)
action (as a verb)
impact (as a verb)
interface (as a verb)
effective and efficient
outcome
output
input
optimal, suboptimal, optimise
minimise
maximise
enhances
cohort
supports (as an all-purpose verb covering all manner of actual or putative actions, such as funding and marketing; as in 'supports the capture of data' and 'supports the product positioning process')
is committed to
utilise (why not 'use'?)
prior (as in 'prior to that' and 'prior year's earnings')
proactive
strategic
facilitate
empower

Redundancies and absurdities

Often these usages are driven by the desire to go one better; stars are trumped by superstars, then by megastars, and then by uberstars. No one can book anymore; we need to pre-book (but would anyone seriously book a thing after it's over?). Then there are those things we write out of habit, but which add nothing.

pre-order
pre-book
stretch goal
forward planning (can there be backward planning?)
currently/current (if you're doing it now, it is by definition current)
negative growth (growth is by definition positive)
going forward (that would be as opposed to going backward)
basically
newly emergent

Statements of the bleeding obvious

It stands to reason that the activities of the organisation will be outcomes-driven, or an employee task-oriented; what we need to know is what those outcomes and tasks are.

outcomes-driven
outcomes-oriented
outcomes-based
evidence-based findings
values-driven
vision-driven
guiding principle
emergent
task-oriented
structured

Oh-so-clever disguises

For when one feels unable or unwilling to call a spade a spade.

reprioritise
rationalisation
reconfigure
liquidity facility (savings account)
take offline
repurpose
open-ended
realign

Crossovers from other genres

Taking a term from one field and applying it in another can be eye-catching and refreshing, but these crossovers often wander into strange and mystical places.

green shoots
blue sky
green fields
organic
sweet spot
ahead of the curve
raise the bar
game plan
anything 2.0
drilling down
signposting
the new black
pipeline
bandwidth
catchment
soup to nuts
game changing
landscape (a thing that, in the real world, is not readily and only gradually changed; as opposed to the 'political landscape', apparently)
leverage(d)
cash lock
on board
on the same page
catching/riding the wave
in the loop
touch base
own goal
pushing the boat out
suck it and see
home run
googly
full toss
hit for six
clean bowled
keystone

Being trendy—by being just like everyone else

Fashionable language like this can look great at first, but by the time everyone adopts a trend, especially one that never had much style, it's already lost its force—not to mention its meaning, if it ever had one.

quick and dirty
laundry list
thinking outside the box
ticking all the boxes
B2C (retail)
B2B (wholesale)
scalable/scaling up, down, anywhere really
funnel down
pushing the envelope
running it up the mast
cascade
embedded
productise
synergy/synergistic
grow (as a verb)
paradigm shift
user-centric
long tail

There are professors, politicians, journalists, managers, sales people, lawyers, scientists and career bureaucrats who'd have nothing to say if you forbade clichés. And, don't tell them we said this, but we'd be no poorer for the silence. What would most managers have left to say if they couldn't use *win–win*, *going forward*, *strategic plan*, *outcome*, *value*, *core deliverables*?

Say what you mean and mean what you say, a famous shrink used to say to his clients, before he sat down and left them to it. Say it plainly, and freshly: you can't mean it, you can't even really know what it is you're saying, if you string it together in someone else's vernacular. Clichés are borrowed, automatic expressions—as opposed to chosen, or deliberate utterances. They are phrases, mostly; they are metaphors, overused and hackneyed, and emptied of life, if not quite of all meaning, even before you take them off the shelf and slot them into a sentence. Clichés are language we can utter without troubling ourselves to think too hard about; we can make a businesslike noise without having to make much sense.

In *1984*, George Orwell parodies as 'duckspeak' the corporate discourse composed mostly of clichés. Noise uttered unconsciously, Orwell's character terms it. Management theorist Stan Glaser, in 'Management Duckspeak', points out how prone executives are to fall for the latest piece of management-speak. Many of us are so easily beguiled by faddish phraseology; we're cliché-struck. 'Give them a new catchphrase', Glaser writes, and too many of them will adopt it, without much critical analysis, as though it were something more than a new articulation of the same old thing—they adopt it as though it will do for the organisation 'what penicillin did to venereal disease'. Language is powerful and seductive. It's easy to fall for the illusion that a new description describes a new phenomenon: philosophers, Glaser reminds us, call this 'the doctrine of misplaced concreteness'. Just because you can name a thing doesn't mean it exists. Too much corporate writing makes this error. And cliché—unconsidered, automatic, fashionable language—is how the error is made; it's how what Glaser calls the 'managerial delusion' is performed. The managerial delusion? Because of the patois they hear and deploy, many managers, says Glaser, mistake an action plan for a strategic plan and a wish list for a strategy; they convince themselves they're managing by giving what they're doing a managerial label.

Here's how Glaser translates a few common organisational expressions:

- empowerment: *asking someone to do something*
- 360 degree feedback: *people talking to each other*
- the learning organisation: *claptrap*.

Here are four big problems with corporate clichés.

- They evacuate and diminish the language.
- They make everything sound like everything else, and nothing like anything in particular.
- They fail your readers (who've heard it all before, and who want to know exactly and only what you and only you mean—and what that means for them).
- Worst of all, they become a way of thinking—which is to say, a way of not thinking, or not very hard or clearly, anyway.

The antidote—not only to clichéd writing but to impoverished thinking—is to question every piece of habitual language that suggests itself; ask yourself, instead, exactly what you really mean, and what that would look like in the real world; then choose some turns of phrase you haven't heard too many times before to express that. Familiar language is good; overfamiliar, bad. Think and speak, in other words, for yourself. Put things the way intelligent readers, impatient for sense, understand them unambiguously—and fast.

We're not talking mostly about technical turns of phrase, many of which you may need to be precise; we mean managerial patois, bureaucratic convolution, false elegance. There is a difference between *outcomes* and *outputs*, between *projects* and *programs*, between *accountability* and *responsibility* (the difference here is illusory and meaningless), between *efficiency* and *effectiveness*, between *goals* and *targets* and *aims*. But if you can't keep hold of the distinction yourself, don't expect your reader to. Use other, more transparent words, or at least define the words before you put them in play. And they're not Siamese twins, either; it's possible to use one of each of the above pairs without necessarily having the other one hold its hand.

Sustainability is another instance of corporate-speak that sounds as if it means more than it does. We all started using it when the ecological implications of our corporate activities started to worry us; people began to speak of the *environmental sustainability* of an activity—whether the activity depleted resources and did such harm to natural systems that it could not be sustained over the long term, if we placed a proper value on the environmental implications. The phrase compelled its users to count and take responsibility for the environmental damage their actions caused—and to stop, if that cost, on some reasonable measure, was too high.

Over the past few years, two things have happened. First, *sustainable* has been co-opted as an adjective to sit beside *economically* and *financially* and other adverbs. Which is fine, except that *sustainable* just means that we can keep doing whatever it is more or less forever; whereas it sounds like something much more moral and robust than that. Second, *environmentally sustainable* has been leached of meaning by overuse; it's too easy to assert and too hard to prove, particularly in theory. So *sustainable* has really come to mean that we'll try not to make too much of a mess, and anyway, we'll be generating jobs.

The moral: ration your clichés. They emasculate your writing; they muddy your thinking; they lose your reader.

A little 'language' may help you seem personable or in the know. But make it a very little.

The other day on the radio an economist said 'Those were the days when anyone who could fog a mirror could get a loan.' That's a cliché in waiting—but not yet a cliché. 'Fog a glass' is an economically expressed and vivid trope. All it says is 'breathe', but the metaphor is colourful and fresh—until every other economist hears it and likes it. Then it will become a cliché fast.

There's an ad on the radio in which someone utters this slogan (about an ecumenical theological college): *Empowering and energising the body of Christ*. That's where cliché can carry you.

5 Business faux pas and how to live them down

Starting sentences with *however* isn't, grammatically speaking, wrong; it's just awkward and inelegant. Not strictly a faux pas. Similarly, corporate clichés, as we've just discussed, and management-speak in general: used uncritically, or overused, they're unhelpful and ungracious, a lapse of taste, but not incorrect.

On the other hand, there are a few old chestnuts that are worth nipping in the bud. *Disinterested* doesn't actually mean *bored* or something like it. That'd be *uninterested*, or *not interested*. *Disinterested* still means what it always did—which is, *objective* or *detached*. In other words, *having no personal, emotional or financial stake in* a case or project or scheme. So, to use the word to mean that blander thing—that we're not interested, thanks—is really a faux pas, no matter how many people don't know that.

While we're at it, nothing can be *quite unique* or *very unique*. No excuses. It's just plain absurd to call something *slightly one-off*. Find another adjective if what you really mean is *different* or *remarkable* or *distinctive* or *special*.

On the other hand, *incidences* and *irregardless* are not—not yet, anyway—words the dictionary is acquainted with. But we read them very often from people who clearly think the words are real. Each is an example of a good word unnecessarily inflated, or two words conflated. *Incident* and its plural *incidents* are good old meaningful words; so are *instance* and *instances*—and *accidents*. *Incidences* is just a confused usage. *Regardless* says everything *irregardless* does; the negative prefix *ir-* doesn't change the meaning of the word. Management likes to add syllables; but don't add anything that adds no meaning—*orient* means what *orientate* means.

Sometimes it seems dictionaries hold the line for as long as they can before eventually, inevitably, succumbing to public pressure and allowing the popular but incorrect usage to take its place at the table. A relatively recent addition is *dissaving*, which is the new term, apparently, for spending.

Having urged you to avoid clichés like the plague, it is perhaps prudent that we also counsel against going too far in the opposite direction and inventing your own language. Coin vivid, shapely phrases, by all means; but favour words already entrenched in the language and try not to mix your metaphors. Access Economics' quarterly *Business Outlook* report of January 2009 advises its readers to *batten the hatches*. 'This is not just a recession', the article goes on. 'This is the sharpest deceleration Australia's economy has ever seen.' It's not the worst example we've ever seen of mixing metaphors, but you batten down the hatches against a brewing storm and rough seas, not when you're travelling in a vehicle (which is unlikely to have hatches to batten down) that is about to pull up sharply. But you might want to check that your seatbelt is tight.

And *unworry* is a bit of a worry. It and its kin are inventive, of course, and memorable. But watch for cheap imitations. The odd neologism is fun, but the language is very large already. So start with the million or more words in the system already.

6 The art of the start

Don't waste the start; it doesn't come again. Don't clear your throat; don't use some corporate platitude. Just get on with it. Find your main point and make it. Or say, at least, why you're writing.

A report starts with an executive summary (see chapter 4) that should arrest the reader and tell them the truth right there; it, too, should start well. Every part of the report will open with an introduction. Don't waste it on waffle; summarise so well your reader won't have to read the chapter. The opening bit of every document—and of every part of every document—is its most important. So begin well, and begin every beginning well.

Further to your letter of, *With reference to*, *Pursuant to* and similar phrases are a kind of bureaucratic cliché. Try these out instead:

> Thank you for your letter/inquiry …
>
> I am writing to …
>
> I enclose our proposal …
>
> In your letter, you asked for guidance … I am delighted to …
>
> In your letter, you raise a number of concerns; let me deal with them one by one.
>
> With this letter I submit our proposal/my application/my resignation …
>
> I am pleased to present our report into the feasibility of a southwest rail link …
>
> I am delighted to apply for this position.
>
> It was good to talk with you this morning. When we spoke you asked about … and I am pleased to be able to let you know that …

Avoid long recitals of government or organisational policy at the start of your correspondence. Don't start with background; start with foreground. Background can wait. Try to address the reader's specific concerns—as you understand them, or as they articulate them in their letter. Get to the point straightaway; in other words, calmly and directly. Where you're composing the same letter for many different readers, try—by adopting a personable tone, by talking, not intoning—not to sound like you're writing a form letter. Never write for a crowd. Write as if you were talking to each reader. Make eye contact and never lose it.

The same rules apply to emails. Indeed, to every kind of business document. Begin with the main point—get to it, at worst, by the second paragraph. And don't waste the start on red tape, formulaic formality and banality; use it to hook them, then draw them in.

7 The art of the close

How you end matters almost as much as how you start. So, don't peter; don't dwindle; don't whimper. Close. Drive home the message; tell them what will happen next or what you hope will happen next; thank them; or just sign off. Enough, already.

Avoid clichéd formalities like *should you have any further queries please do not hesitate to contact…* Many business writers seem to feel obliged to write that, or something like it; it's in many template letters. But you don't have to say it; you don't have to say anything—except what you mean. If your letter is clear, stop writing and sign off, pointing the way ahead perhaps. (Indeed, *should you have any further queries* implies you're not sure whether—or you couldn't be bothered making sure that—you've addressed the reader's concerns.)

Every letter, every document, will want to close in its own way, depending on what it says and what you want to do next, but here are some sample closes you might like to add to your list.

> Let me know if I can help you further.
>
> I look forward to talking with you about the proposal/job/project … when we meet.
>
> I'll call you next week to arrange a time to …

We're excited about working with you on this job; we look forward to the next step.

This report makes recommendations of significance to the lives and livelihoods of all Australians. We're pleased to have had the chance to write it, and we offer it in the hope that it will make a difference.

But whatever it is, make it clear and trim and personable. This is the last thing you say to them—so make it pay.

8 Non-attachment

You often use a letter or an email to cover another document—your application and resumé, the proposal, the contract, the report. The attached or enclosed document, not the letter, is often the main game, the real deal. So how you phrase the 'attached please find' bit counts.

Attached is and *please find attached* are the most common articulations, and both are passive and unnecessarily formal these days. Just add *herewith* and you're back in the era and the diction Charles Dickens parodied so well so long ago in *Bleak House* (1853). Try something a bit less uptight:

I attach ...

Here is ...

Our proposal details this fully.

9 Fooling yourself

If you want to write well, you need to relax. You need to ease back because good writing sounds easy and cool (unlike the struggle it always is). You need to relax because anxiety is the enemy of clarity and sense and economy. When you're ill at ease, you'll clam up or bang on; you'll evade and dissemble and copy the most conforming, least relaxed examples of others.

Anxiety afflicts professional writers, too. You can think way too hard and long about the fact that this is a poem you want to write, a book review, an essay, a story, or, god help you, a book; the more you think of the writing that way, the less like writing it becomes. If you want to write a poem, think of it as a tweet. If you want to write an annual report, think of it as a shopping list.

Now, if relaxing at the keyboard is your idea of hard work, try fooling yourself. Convincing your psyche you're not writing at all—that what your fingers are doing is what your mouth sometimes does well when you're talking with someone you trust about something you know—is most of the game of writing well. Here's one good way to perform the trick.

Whatever you have to write—especially if it's a big proposal, a job application, a paper, a speech—open your email program, not Microsoft Word. Address an email to a good friend. Try explaining to them what you're working on and what you've decided about it.

Tell your friend your thesis and how you got to it; describe your approach; summarise the findings; write the whole thing, if you like. Writing to someone you know feels less like writing and more like talking. Let it relax you; let it help you think and speak clearly. Forget, while you write, whom your piece is really for. You can remind yourself of that later and perform a little minor surgery.

By writing a letter to a friend, you may write the best policy proposal or thesis or business case you're ever likely to write.

Oh, and don't send the email (in fact, best to do it in Draft mode in case you sneeze and hit Send). Copy it into a Word document and take it from there.

10 Making yourself ready to write

Don't write without a map. Either you'll get lost, or your reader will. But don't make the map too tidy. Don't make it a list, for instance. A mindmap is what you need—that looser and wilder kind of chart of the way there.

But in truth, a mindmap doesn't so much map your document as make you ready to write it. It pulls you out of the thick of the detail; it gives you some perspective; it lets you see the five (or twenty-five) points you're making out of all that research and thought, and the one thesis they all amount to. The mindmap is a loose, impressionistic chart of the mind that's going to be making the case to the fingers that will be taking it down. A writer can be—maybe even should be—messy in many other respects, but she should be tidy in this one. She should be across her story. Right down to its moral.

Chapter 6 of *The Little Red Writing Book* has some more to say about this.

11 I'm okay; you're okay

There's an idea about that you never write *I* in business. It's time to move on from that slender fallacy. You may not need *I* very often, but sometimes you will, and where you do, you should use it. The bias against the personal pronoun is one of the chief reasons so much organisational and professional writing is so bad—so stuffy and stilted, so awkward and passive and abstract and voiceless. So unclear. Outlawing *I* is an element of a project at which too many of us have connived: stripping functional writing of its human qualities, an ideology and a fallacy about which writers from George Orwell to Don Watson have fulminated compellingly. Bureaucracies that pretend they are not composed of people doing jobs, and that you're not a person either; organisations that reify, almost deify, processes and retreat behind them are falsifying reality, emasculating language and alienating us all—those whom at the same moment they often say they wish to delight or empower.

If you're writing the letter and you have cause to refer to yourself (*I write to inform you*; *I took your proposal to the publishing committee, but, alas, they rejected it*; *Let me answer your questions one by one*; *I attach the brochures you asked about*; *I am pleased to apply for the job*; *Please call me if I can help you further*), you'll need, as a matter of grammar, the first personal pronoun: *I*. As a matter of law, the person signing the letter or email has the authority they are charged with (under contract of employment, usually as expressed under the signature); they are the agent of the enterprise. If you're writing the paper or the thesis, guess what? These are your conclusions; this is you, here, telling us what you've found and what you make of that. You'll be as considered and objective as you possibly can; these are not, after all, your glib and uncritical remarks. *I* doesn't mean *merely personal*; it means *the writer*. The writer who very often speaks for the school, the state, the department or the firm, as its agent; but an individual writerly self, all the same. You, if you're writing it, which is to say *I*.

I isn't ever wrong—you just won't need it much. There are times, for instance, when you as the writer don't actually speak the document. Often in functional writing, a virtuous fiction is at play: the audit report is understood to be written by the audit office—well, in theory by the auditor-general—when in fact it's the work of two or three auditors; the proposal, though penned by you, is made, just as the work it tenders for will be performed, by your whole organisation; legislation, though drafted by one or more legal draftspeople, speaks the mind, as it were, of the state; policy speaks the mind of the institution. In other cases, such as media releases and newsletter entries and in journalism itself, the writer employs the detached third-person point of view to tell a story that isn't normally *about* himself. So, you won't use *I* in such documents—not because it's wrong, but because you have no occasion to refer to yourself as the utterer of that text.

On the other hand, you write speeches for yourself or someone else to give; the speaker will need to refer to themselves, and when they do they'll say *I*: *I have a dream*; *There are three things I know about business writing*.

In job applications and resumés, where the writer is also the hero of the story, the first person is fine. As we mentioned, many people drop *I* and write odd bureaucratic sentence fragments; others cast themselves in the third person. But *I* is the easier and more logical, so use it. In letters and emails, it belongs, too: you're talking to your readers, here; your name's on the top or the bottom, so the voice and the ideas it speaks are yours.

I write on behalf of the minister to let you know …

Although a line of narrow thinking has hardened into a dogma that scientific and scholarly papers and theses should never use *I*, the best ones do. And why not? Objectivity isn't achieved by leaving yourself out of the writing and pretending these are not your thoughts. Indeed, such documents are meant to be nothing more or less than articulations of the writer's sustained and critical thinking on a subject. Objectivity is a function of thinking, not of diction. Write yourself modestly back in; take ownership of your thinking and your conclusions. Pretending they are not there doing the research, applying the logic, drawing conclusions and expressing them circumspectly leads writers to all sorts of unproductive and unedifying convolutions. The reader also gets the feeling this artifice of self-abnegation is a place to hide: the writer has nothing to say that hasn't been said before, so they gloss the literature and that's about it.

Charles Darwin, father of modern science, wrote very naturally and dispassionately in the first person. Now, if it was good enough for him, the foremost scientist of the modern era, maybe it's good enough for all the scientists and the managers, professionals, scholars and report writers who have adopted scientific method in their writing. Just maybe we could wean ourselves off false objectivity and try some actual, humane detachment.

But there are alternatives to *I* (or if there are two or more of you, *we*) in papers and theses: *This paper/this thesis/this study argues*; *The data shows*; *Our research revealed...*

Scholarly and technical writers often turn to the passive voice to keep themselves out of their writing and affect objectivity. But don't go there, at least not often. The passive voice has its problems, all listed and unpacked in *The Little Red Writing Book*: it sounds sneaky (Richard Nixon's *Mistakes have been made* shows you how), even when you don't mean it to; it sounds stiff, even pompous (*it is recommended that changes in her behaviour be addressed*); it's dull because it hides the agent of the action, the doer of the deed, and strips your sentences of action; it's vague because (as in *further research will be undertaken*) it fails to sheet home responsibility for the verb; and it's inefficient—the passive voice uses more syllables to say the same thing, or less than the same thing, as the active (*we will undertake further research* tells you more than *further research will be undertaken* in one less syllable; if you add *by us* to the passive sentence, it gets longer still).

> Please be informed that a decision was reached at the meeting held yesterday in respect of your application.
>
> Your proposal in response to the call for expressions of interest has been considered and judged to be in accord with the aims of the organisation.
>
> It is the recommendation of the agency that better practices in the maintenance of prescription records in this respect be implemented in all healthcare centres with a view to the minimisation of patient harm as a consequence of suboptimal prescription.

So, there's no blanket ban on the first-person pronoun at work. Use it when it occurs to you. In fact, things will go more honestly and humanely when more of us start acknowledging our presence in the documents we write.

12 Spelling it out

Abbreviations and acronyms plague functional writing. Keep a lid on them. They're ugly, and they're hard work to read. They may save you some trouble, but they cause it for your reader. So, if in doubt, spell the thing out. Don't imagine that a good glossary, or a translation offered the first time you employ the phrase for which the acronym stands in, excuses you from employing the full phrase. Readers forget, and it's not especially polite to force them to keep consulting the glossary. In a longer document, repeat the full phrase at its first mention in every chapter.

And try more relaxed abbreviations—abbreviations that are themselves words. Instead of *DIAC* for the *Department of Immigration and Citizenship*, you could write *the department*; instead of *FBE* for *the Faculty of Business and Economics*, try *the faculty*. You could refer to *The Little Black Book of Business Writing* as *TLBBBW*, which is handy, but ugly, or as *the book* or *the little black book*, which are much more reader-friendly uses.

The convention is to use the full text the first time, with your abbreviation (especially if it's an acronym) in parentheses beside it. You don't have to do that if you're going to go for something more generic, and much more relaxed and readable (like *the department*, or *the book*). Of course, substituting *the department* for *DIAC* throughout a document that involves several other departments won't work so well (unless you use acronyms for all the others). So, be sensible but subtle. Acronyms aren't, as many business writers seem to believe, compulsory. Use as few as you can.

Acronyms seem to be on the rise, a plague on all our houses. The 2009 review of the performance of the Strategic Indigenous Housing and Infrastructure Program (SIHIP), for instance, begins with a listing of abbreviations and acronyms, an ominous sign, but at least we're forewarned—and forearmed. Some of the reductions are obviously helpful—*SIHIP*, for a start—but the value of abbreviations such as *IPT* (Integrated Program Team) and *PSR* (Package Scoping Report) is less certain.

As we write, we have a prime minister (make that PM) who's caught the acronym habit something bad. When asked by a journalist in 2008 if NATO (an abbreviation we're used to, and which most of us would understand without being able to spell out) leaders had changed the rules of engagement applying to NATO soldiers, the prime minister responded, 'You mean RoEs.' At least that one had been defined, but the prime minister is equally fond of the undefined acronym. In the weeks following the RoE news conference, the PM used the acronyms *EWS* (early warning system), *IFIs* (international financial institutions), *RTPs* (rights to protect) and *CCS* (carbon capture and storage), before achieving a PB (personal best) with *CSBMs* (confidence and security-building measures).

13 Capitalising

Outside headings and acronyms, use an initial capital only with proper nouns. So, for most of your theories and isms, job titles, boards and committees, and minutes, papers and procedures, you can put those capital letters back in your pocket. Far fewer things need capitals than we find uses for. To overcapitalise is not a capital offence; it's just a little uncool.

People's real names are proper nouns. So, too, place names, company names, property names, river names, product names, book titles (which should also be written in italic). Job titles can be proper nouns, too, but it depends. If you want to, you can write *Eduardo Galeano, Manager—People and Development*; and *Melissa Ho, Chief Executive Officer*. But you can (indeed should, if you put it this way) write: *the manager of people and development, Eduardo Galeano*; and *the company's chief executive officer, Melissa Ho*. (If you use *our* (or another possessive adjective) or an article (*the* or *a/an*) or *the company's* in front of the title, you are, by definition, using the title as a common noun—one commonly occurring. So, even *President Kennedy* was *the president* (although *the President of the United States of America* is the normal usage for that particular office).

Military, church, teaching, medical and state titles are usually proper nouns: *General*, *Archbishop*, *Rinpoche*, *Guru*, *Roshi*, *Brother*, *Mother*, *Sister*, *Professor*, *Vice-chancellor*, *Judge*, *Detective Sergeant*, *Minister*, *Prime Minister* and *President*. But they are only proper nouns when accompanied by the name of the particular general, pope, teacher or priest: *General Custer*, *Pope Pius*, *Trungpa Rinpoche*, *Minister Brown*. Otherwise, it's meant to be *the general*, *the pope*, *the rinpoche*, *the vice-chancellor*, *the minister*; but usage varies, and some people like capitals for some of these. We assume there's only one Pope, just as there is only one Dalai Lama; but there is never only one minister, lieutenant or professor.

The same dignity is not bestowed in sport: you don't write *Half-back Billy Smith*, *Opening Batter Sally Bowls*. You might write *World Champion Layne Beachley*, that being a bigger deal than half-back or opening bat. But it's not really required. Nor would you need initial caps for musical titles, such as *conductor* (though *Maestro*, by convention, would be capitalised along with the conductor's full or family name), *principal violinist*, *mezzo-soprano* and so on. And you wouldn't write *Poet and Mystic Jalal ad-Din Muhammad Rumi*.

It ought to follow that corporate titles, like *General Manager*, *Chairwoman* and *HR Manager*, should not need initial caps, but they generally get them, one supposes, by analogy with offices of state and church. But remember not to bother with the cap when you're writing *the chairwoman*, *our manager of human resources*, *a sales representative*, or *customer services executive*.

Board, as in *the board of directors*, oughtn't take a capital either, but it normally does. *Government* requires a cap only when it's used as a noun as part of the full title of the particular government: *Victorian Government*, *Rudd Government*, *Australian Government*. You don't use a cap *G* when *government* is used as an adjective: *government policy*, *government offices*. *Minister*, though it doesn't need a cap *M* in *the Minister's office*, often gets one.

Doctrines or schools of thought, such as *capitalism*, *democracy*, *postmodernism*, *libertarianism*, don't need caps. But schools of religious thought normally do: *Buddhism*, *Gnosticism*, *Islam*, *Hindu*, *Zen*, *Taoism*, *Christianity*, *Protestantism*.

And although disciplines or fields of study, like *law*, *accounting*, *history*, *geography*, *marketing*, *publishing*, *science*, *biology* and *project management*, don't need caps, you can use an initial cap to denote that narrower, professional meaning where there is also another general meaning, with which there might be some confusion: *you'll find History in building 6FC*; but *there is a history of abuse*.

But this is getting messy. There's a simple rule, despite the many exceptions and the inclination of corporate, professional, academic and bureaucratic writers to want to dignify functions, processes, concepts and titles with capitals. In general, don't put a cap on a noun if you're using it as a common noun, which you are if you precede it with a determiner: *the minister*, *the government of the day*, *the leader*, *the professor*, *the policy*, *our hospital*, *the auditor-general*. And no matter how important the concept or idea is to you and your case, it doesn't warrant a capital unless it's religious!

But there is scope, as ever, for difference. There are minimal and maximal capitalisers. The more you love words, it seems, the less you like capitals; the more you love politics, the more you like capitals.

Everything we've said applies to words used in full text; headings are a special case. And with headings you can do pretty much what you like. Capitals in headings are a matter of design, not usage. You can capitalise every letter of every word, if you like, for impact; or every initial letter of every word; or only the initial letter of the first word (and any proper nouns); or even none at all. The rule here is consistency. Settle on a style for every level of heading, and apply it doggedly.

14 Use verbs—plenty of them, mostly active

Verbs are the doing words. They act; they animate; they activate. Without one, you don't have a sentence, and you don't have a story. Without a verb, nothing happens.

Good writing is rich with verbs. Good writing, yes even in the functional realm, favours the kinds of verb in which life as we experience it enacts itself over and over: *changes*, *adopts*, *adapts*, *lifts*, *rises*, *falls*, *points out*, *says*, *runs*, *reads*, *notes*, *makes sure*, *finds*, *finds out*, *looks into*, *concludes*, *creates*, *draws*, *writes*, *nourishes*, *encourages*, *constrains*, *shows*, *blinds*, *closes*, *opens*, *shuts*, *leads*, *files*, *harnesses*, *carries*, *teaches*, *learns*, *condemns*, *praises*, *limits*, *rations*, *fulfils*, *starts*, *stops*, *wants*, *needs*, *demands*, *finishes*. That sort of thing.

Writing replete with verbs of this kind—for reasons elaborated in *The Little Red Writing Book* and having to do with the basic *who does what* of sentences—will always feel more alive and lifelike. Something always happens in a sentence with that kind of verb in it; there'll be an actor and an action; there'll be a story that goes the way life seems to a reader to go, in the flesh. Such prose can't fail to engage a reader. Unlike classic bureaucratic, managerial, academic and scientific writing, which abjures such verbs and avoids human beings (and other concrete entities) wherever it can, favouring instead the verb *to be* (*is*, *are*, *were*, *will be*, *will have been* ...) and verbs expressed in the passive voice, and nominalising (turning into nouns) whatever verbs it might have employed—rendering its sentences inanimate and making them almost impossible for a reader to engage with, let alone understand.

> It is a recommendation of the report that implementation of strategic responses conducive to a learning environment be prioritised and prosecuted with expedition across the institution.

> It is proposed that a working group be established to explore the possibility of setting up a committee to examine the appropriate way

to assimilate the various stakeholders' views that impact on the overall activities of the organisation moving forward.

Compliance with the applicable legislation and conformity with relevant accounting standards are studied across the sample organisations.

Instead of the gutsy little verbs good writers favour, much business writing, where it turns to verbs apart from *to be* at all, privileges such abstract, polysyllabic, anemic, pretentious doing words as these: *enhances, supports, facilitates, actions, indicates, initiates, implements, integrates, develops, demonstrates, comprises, advances, enables, empowers, inculcates, utilises, maximises, minimises, optimises, rationalises, necessitates, expedites, precludes, predicates, notifies, requires, ensures, allocates, segments.*

It is also committed to vague, elongating verb phrases such as *committed to, is aligned with, is consistent with, has responsibility for, has oversight of, is comprised of, is indicative of.*

If you want to trim, smarten and enrich your business prose, gather up as many small, good, real verbs as you can, set them down in sound sentences after some real-life (human, or humanoid) subjects, and keep those verbs active. Do everything the classic bureaucratic sentence doesn't. Write a little like this, for instance:

Our research shows that when doctors and other health professionals adopt good-quality decision support in prescribing drugs, health outcomes improve significantly for patients.

The SEC regulates corporate behaviour, enforces corporations and securities legislation, and administers policies designed to encourage and sustain efficient securities markets in Australia.

In May 2008, the IASB established an external expert advisory panel to look at whether and how fair value reporting contributed to the global financial crisis.

We deliver what we promise.

15 Write out loud

The most useful thing to remember at the keyboard is this: write like you talk, only better. And the best trick we know to make sure you do that is to write out loud.

Write with your ears, not just your eyes and fingers. Words don't sit silently on the paper; they speak. And it would be good if they spoke the sounds you meant them to speak to make the meaning you meant them to make.

To help your writing talk, and to help tidy that talk into the best kind of writing, sound out your sentences as you set them down. Or write, if you must, in silence, but make sure you read your writing out loud to yourself once you think you've got it down.

Reading it out loud may be the best way to edit your writing and to practise on it the care it's impossible to take while you're drafting it. It's the best way, if you listen hard, and if you make yourself hard to please, to test your thinking, and catch yourself in grammatical error, and generally to make sure your writing talks in the intelligent vernacular to someone like yourself—only less patient and less inclined to forgive you for cant and abstraction.

Never send a piece of writing into the world without sounding it out first.

16 Earn your conclusions

Making a proposal, writing a report or a thesis, writing a strategy, teaching a class, even selling a product, you're making an argument. Argument is one of the four modes of rhetoric (the others are description, narration and exposition, and all of them play a part in business writing). You don't win an argument—you don't make a case—by assertion. When you argue, Mark wrote in *The Little Red Writing Book*, 'you put a case and defend it, by use, especially, of logic.'

Too few business documents, including especially academic papers and theses, earn their conclusions: they argue by repeated assertion rather than by thesis. You make a thesis, another name for an argument, by proposing a hypothesis and testing it by critical thought, evidence and experiment, until you're left with a claim (thesis) that stands up; you argue by making a claim and justifying it—by putting a case and making it—through a combination of evidence, reasoning and persuasive language. You assert a thing and you prove it. But you earn your conclusion by the calibre of your proof.

Evidence includes

- empirical data gathered from reputable sources (treasury numbers, World Health Organization and UN figures, bureau of statistics stats, documented scientific research and so on)
- data you gather yourself through qualitative and quantitative research
- the results of your own experiments
- personal testimony—your own and that of reliable witnesses
- anecdotes and case studies
- expert opinion (expressed in books and articles), critically assessed and weighed, in the case of conflicting opinions, carefully.

Instead of critically analysing expert opinion, weighing both sides of a debate, or even making a case themselves by logic, unsophisticated academic theses and government reports proffer the views of one or two authorities as evidence for a claim. This won't do it. Argue with the authorities, test them, weigh them, assess them: nothing is lore.

Here are a couple of instances of logical reasoning.

> On 10 November 2008, the leader of the opposition said in parliament, 'the government went to the electorate with a proposal to scrap the workplace reform legislation I supported when we drafted and enacted it

in government. The government won the election and it won a mandate to scuttle the legislation. We need to respect that.' Now, the leader of the opposition opposes the government's legislation to scuttle the conservatives' workplace reforms and replace them with fairer legislation. The leader of the opposition is a hypocrite; or he has changed his mind and opposition policy in order to preach to his unruly backbench.

All swans are white [a false premise as philosophers discovered when Europeans discovered Australia]; these swan-like birds are black; so, these birds cannot be swans.

In its charter, the agency commits itself to plain English. Tested on focus groups of the agency's clients, the agency's brochure on the new process for lodging applications received overwhelmingly negative feedback to the effect that it was almost impossible to understand and use in making applications. In addition, an audit by the Plain English unit at the London School of Economics (LSE) rated the brochure 2 out of 10 for readability. Assuming the agency retains its professed commitment to plain English; assuming also the agency continues to believe that clarity of expression is a virtue in the public service it performs, it should withdraw the brochure and issue a new one, tested first on focus groups and audited by the LSE to make sure it speaks in a language the readers of the document can understand.

Unearned conclusions sound like what they are: bald assertions. Learn to evidence and argue elegantly for and write with quiet persuasion about the claims and promises you make.

17 Avoiding apostrophe catastrophes

The apostrophe is still in use, and the rules are still the same.

An apostrophe has only two uses in contemporary English—in business, science, government, advertising, scholarship, legislation, poetry, the works. No exceptions.

- It marks letters missing in contractions, like *can't*, *isn't*, *you'll* and *they're*.

- It indicates, followed by the letter *s* (*'s*), the possessive form of nouns: *Geoff's idea*, *the company's profits*, *the experiment's main outcomes*, *your reader's needs*.

It's hard to say why the apostrophe causes so much confusion. For more on all this, see *The Little Green Grammar Book*. Here's a summary.

1. Never use an apostrophe to make a noun plural. That's not a job the apostrophe does; *s* or *es* or some other suffix (*children* for more than one child; *dice* for more than one *die*) does that. So all of these are wrong when used as plurals (and thousands of others like them): *thousand's*, *the Roche's*, *pyjama's*, *apple's*, *university's*/*universitie's*, *supplier's*/*suppliers'*.
2. Abbreviations (like *CD* and *PDF*) don't need an apostrophe, either, to turn them into their plural; just add an *s*: *DVDs*, *CDs*, *PDFs*, *PHDs*, *KPIs*.
3. Making a plural of *do* and worse still *don't* can get ugly with an apostrophe. Put *do* and *don't* in italic, thus: *do*s and *don't*s.
4. For the years of the 1960s or 1990s, or any other decades, whether you use numerals or words, use no apostrophe either (since this is another instance of the plural): *1960s*, *sixties*, *1990s*, *nineties*. When the usage is *sixties music* or *60s music*, there's still no apostrophe. *Sixties* and *60s* would be regarded as adjectives.
5. Many people regard these usages (*womens*, *mens*, *childrens*, *writers* and *mothers*) as correct without an apostrophe on the same grounds they can be regarded as adjectives: *The Royal Womens Hospital*, *Mens shirts*, *Westmead Childrens Hospital*, *the NSW Writers Centre*. But others argue for the apostrophe: *The Royal Women's Hospital*, *Men's shirts*, *Westmead Children's Hospital*, *the NSW Writer's Centre, Mother's Day*.
6. Since *children* is the plural of *child*, *the childrens' nanny* doesn't make any sense; that'd be *the children's nanny*. Similarly, *womens' hospital* and *mens' business* just can't be right; they should be *women's hospital* and *men's*

business, since it's the *women* and the *men*, not the *womens* and the *mens*, who are doing the possessing.

7 Some people argue that it should be *Writers' Centre* and *Mothers' Day*, as in the centre of (as in *for* or *belonging to*) all writers, and the day of all mothers.

8 When the noun of possession is plural (that is, when you mean that more than one company or reader or writer or employee or experiment or owner ... owns something) and ends in an *s*, drop the *s* after the apostrophe: *the companies' assets*, *your readers' needs*, *my parents' house*, *all our employees' wages and conditions*, *the horses' tails*, *the directors' shareholdings*.

9 Where a noun doesn't take an *s* or *es* in its plural form, add an apostrophe and an *s* when you use it possessively: *the mice's whiskers*, *the data's significance*, *the dice's rattle*.

10 *Its* is the possessive form (some grammarians call it a possessive adjective) of the pronoun *it* (just as *my* is the possessive of *I* and *his* of *he* and *her* of *she* and *your* of *you*). By contrast, *it's* is a contraction of *it is*. So it's *The company complies with its obligations*, and *It's a legal matter*.

11 Use the apostrophe to make the possessive forms of all given names and family names, including those that end in *s*: *Rachel's proposal*, *Nina's voice*, *James's contribution*, *Chris's calculations*, *Joseph Banks's book*, *Wallace Stevens's theory*.

12 Some people make an exception of *Jesus*: *Jesus' disciples*. Not that this may come up too often.

13 Apostrophes of possession may be dropped these days in the names of suburbs, churches and schools: *St Geoffreys*, *St Beatrices*, *St Pauls Cathedral*, *Quakers Hill*, *Coffs Harbour*.

14 If in doubt, check it out. Where, for instance, there's room for variation, check whether the organisation uses an apostrophe in its own materials, and do what they do: is it *St James Ethics Centre* or *St James's*

Ethics Centre or *St James' Ethics Centre*? How do they name themselves on their website and documents? Is it *The Womens College* or *the Womens College*, *The Women's College* or *the Women's College*? Is it *McDonald's* or *McDonalds*?

18 The good word guide

There is probably a time for every usage under heaven. Including some of those in the left-hand column below. But because they're small and good and unpretentious; because the short works faster and more honestly than the long (even a string of short words is better than a single long or prim bureaucratic banality); because the particular is better than the vague, the concrete better than the abstract; and because, by now, you'd rather be clear than meekly conforming, favour the words on the right.

RATION	**PREFER**
a majority of	most
a number of	many [or say how many]
above or abovementioned	[avoid; try 'this' or 'the']
absence of	no, none
accommodation(s)	room, hotel, digs
adjustments	changes
afforded an opportunity to	allowed, let
aggregate [noun or verb]	total
albeit	even though, even if she is
as a consequence of	because of
ascertain	find out, make sure
assist/assistance	help, aid, guide/help, aid, guidance
bottom line	gist, what this amounts to, thesis
by virtue of	because
capability	talent, ability

RATION	PREFER
commence/commencement	start, begin/start, beginning
competency	skill, ability
component	part
comprising/is comprised of	including
concerning	about
connectivity	[must we?]
consequent upon	because of
consequently	so
contained in	in
deficiency	lack
designate	appoint, point out, set up
despite the fact that	even though
disposal	sale
driver	factor, reason, element, agent
due to the fact that	because
e.g. [a Latin abbreviation]	for example
ensure	make sure
etc. [Latin abbreviation for et cetera]	[avoid by introducing a list with 'including']
expiration	end
facilitate	help, lead, run
facility	ease, gift, office, washroom, hospital ...
has the capability to	can
has the potential to	might
i.e. [a Latin abbreviation]	—, :, that is
impact [verb]	affect, change, hamper, bolster
in excess of	more than
in respect of	about, on
in the event that	if
information resources centre	library
intent	aim, plan
interface	meet, work together, join, marry

RATION	PREFER
is entitled to	may
lengthy	long
maximise	enlarge, get the most out of, fulfil
minimise	limit, reduce, dismiss
modality	means, form, mode
motivation	cause, reason
necessitate	cause, compel
on each occasion when	whenever
on the grounds that	because
optimise	get the most from, improve
partially	partly
preorder	order, book
prior to	before
prioritise	rank, list, order, set priorities
procurement	sourcing, buying, leasing …
provide	give
rationalise	fix, straighten out, trim, sort out
refurbish	fit out, mend, repair, paint
request	ask
several	[be specific about how many; name them …]
should you wish	if you want
staff	people
state [the problem here is not the word but its tireless use, as in 'the commission's report stated', 'the new CEO stated today'; 'Barthes states that']	say, advise, write, note, conclude, observe
strategise	think, plan, prepare
suboptimal	imperfect, flawed
subsequent to	after
support	[largely redundant, but sometimes] fund, serve, service

RATION	PREFER
sustained an injury to (her right arm)	injured (her right arm)
twenty-four/seven	non-stop; all day, every day; always
until such time as	until
utilisation	use
variation	change
vehicle	car, truck, motorbike ...
with regard to	about

Our list is incomplete; that's the problem. The trick of it is resisting the orthodox and testing yourself to come up with everyday words and phrases, clear and concrete substitutes for all such empty, clichéd usages.

CHAPTER 6

BEAUTY IS TRUTH—LEADERSHIP, VIRTUE AND GOOD PROSE STYLE

A small rant against cant

This book has put the case for clear and graceful writing at work, and in the public space. We've tried to show, through how we've written, through tips and tools and tutelage, how you might—by courage and technique—lift your writing game in whatever line of business you're in.

But we have a loftier ambition, too. This book, we dare to hope, may help you, in your small way—shaping lovelier, leaner, more useful and efficient sentences on the shop floor or at the coalface, against a tight deadline—to smarten up, deepen and enliven the conversation in which society defines and improves itself, transacts business and keeps itself honest. 'Be generous with the truth', *The Little Red Writing Book* suggested, 'and economical with how you tell it. Most of us do it the other way round; that is the art of politics. Mean as much as you can in the fewest syllables; that is the art of writing.'

It's the art of leadership, too. Not to mention good business and good governance. So much depends on having something to say—preferably something worth saying—and saying it, and not something roughly like it, or something else, or nothing meaningful at all.

All of this is only worth saying—and we are far from the first to say it—because we seem to have tripped ourselves up into an era of bad language. We live in an age of cant and spin and verbiage. Language—that meaningful vernacular music we are meant to use to make sense of the world and our places in it, to buy groceries and sell our old jeans and cutting-edge services on the internet, to get our work done, to wonder and chant and play and pray and grieve and plan and remember and report and confess and love—language is too often, these days, subterfuge.

Sometimes the subterfuge is deliberate; mostly it's an accident of uncritical adoption of bad writing habits that seem to have hardened into orthodoxy in schools and churches, businesses and bureaucracies. At least as often as it's used to explain something, language is strained, in the workplace and the marketplace, in the parliament and the media, in the classroom and the courtroom, to bully and dissemble; to pose and mislead; to buy time and fill space; to say as little as we can, over and again; to cover our back; to conform rather than to elucidate; and to baffle.

What is said is hardly ever meant; or if it was meant, it's hard to work out exactly what that meaning was anyway. And what is meant is hardly ever said—for want of skill and, just as often, courage. Being clear scares the hell out of most people who have to write—which is almost enough to guarantee that most of the writing you see around you will be opaque and evasive. As well as the techniques and the disciplines of writerly care this book has laid out, clarity of expression demands clarity of mind, a quality not equally distributed, let's be frank, and easily disturbed by the exigencies of everyday life and work; and it demands a little courage, too.

Too often, if it is not subterfuge, writing is pretension. Setting aside those people anxiously doing their best to manufacture meaning employing models hopelessly inadequate for the business of saying a lot with a little, too many functional writers, instead of writing, spend their precious time at the keyboard advertising their expertise, or trying to sound like someone who sounds like they know what they're talking about, or saving themselves the trouble of thinking straight or saying anything they might be held accountable for—by discoursing in desiccated polysyllables (such as those last ones).

This book is what to do instead. And why. And how.

You'd want to write—wouldn't you?—the way you'd like democracy to run. Or, a happy family; an efficient market. Words are *not* cheap—not words carefully chosen, truthful and gracefully voiced. Good societies speak forth good societies; good societies speak and demand good sentences. A country's politics and culture—its national conversation—are about as healthy and humane as its prose; and from what we read in the public domain, it seems we're in a bit of trouble. But all we need to right the ship is the courage and technique to make sentences that are worthy of us, that add to the stock of wisdom, if not joy. And so the struggle to improve our sentences is also the struggle to improve ourselves.

In 'How to Understand the Disaster', published in the *New York Times Review of Books* on 14 May 2009, an essay that enacts the art of writing simply about great complexity, Robert Solow notes:

> I once saw a hospital discharge diagnosis that read 'sepsis of unknown etiology'; that sort of thing will not do in this case.

The 'case' he has in mind is coming to some understanding of how the global financial crisis of 2008 came about, so that we might avoid another like it. What is required is some clear thinking and some plain speaking—such as that he models in the essay. The best that can be said for the phrase he critiques is that it is an expert discourse, uttered without regard for any but very narrow needs, and unlikely to add to the general stock of knowledge. For two reasons: its diction ('sepsis' and 'etiology') is arcane; it discovers and articulates no cause.

If tin-eared, recondite language like this, written without regard for the humanity of its audience (in this case, presumably, other medical staff), is sometimes excusable because it employs the dialect of the tribe, it remains, nonetheless, pompous and rather silly.

It's hard to think of any excuse, though, for this:

> Relationships with and between learners are initiated which support inclusivity, acknowledge diversity and enable a positive learning environment.

No, we didn't make that up; someone running TAFE did that, or some bright and expensive consultant they hired to help them write their policy on teaching and learning. The pomposity here isn't justified in this case by the narrowness of the discourse: this sentence is meant to help teachers teach. Apart from its manifest silliness, it's hard to think of a rule of writing style and common sense it doesn't break. If such writing has become conventional around you, so much the worse; all the more reason to resist. The question is how we could have allowed such writing to get hold; why do we tolerate it and reward those who coin and parrot it?

If how we write is who we are, we very often look pretty silly, and we'd better start doing something about the kind of writing that makes us so.

Apart from anything else, this is not the language of leadership or democracy; it's bureaubabble. And what is it doing—of all places—in an institution of learning? What is it meant to teach?

Once, the local pool was called, for instance, 'Leichhardt Pool' or 'the baths'; now, it's likely to be called on the signage and in the local government documents 'Leichhardt Aquatic Leisure Centre'. This sets a bad example to the young. A submission to the Montara Commission of Inquiry into the big oil spill that occurred in the Timor Sea in 2009 referred to what had happened as 'an uncontrolled hydrocarbon release'. Those who have committed a crime are just as likely to find themselves 'assigned to a boutique correctional facility' as sentenced to jail. If, when buying an apartment, you can't afford the penthouse, give some thought to the next level down—consider a 'sub-penthouse apartment'. Despite the lessons that should have been learned about language from the Victorian bushfires of 2009, we are still being told by the authorities, when the weather turns hot, the wind rises and the humidity falls, that we face 'a very difficult weather scenario'.

And we have at present a prime minister given to such usages as 'the sea–beach interface', which is apparently what most of us had previously known as the shore.

This is getting silly. Let's start again, and do it right. How we write our signage is how we teach our students and how we treat our sick and how, finally, we rule ourselves. It's time to do all this differently. Time for a bit more intelligence and grace.

What we write at work doesn't have to be fancy, and it shouldn't be flash. But this is business (or something professional, like scholarship or bureaucracy or law) we're doing here, so we'd want our writing to sound as though we'd applied some robust business principles—like thrift and attention to detail, a little deft benchmarking, a bit of contemplation of consumer need—to the making of it.

Here's part of an annual report written by a bank in 1957. There's no poetry on show here; but more to the point, there's no spin or babble. It uses unfussy everyday verbs like *rose*, *stood* and *called*. Its sentences, which run both short and long, cohere; so do its paragraphs. It lays the facts and context out plainly.

> During 1956–57 total assets rose by 22 million pounds and at 30 June 1957 stood at 252 million pounds. Customer accounts increased by 34,000 to 549,000. The bank extended its representation to 64 new centres, and we now provide banking facilities at 525 branches and 79 agencies throughout Australia, Papua New Guinea, the British Solomon Islands and London.
>
> The bank maintained a very liquid position through the year, reflecting the expansion that occurred in Australia's overseas trading. Deposits rose by 17 million pounds.

> The Central Bank called an additional 8 million pounds to Special Account during the year, and a total of 39.2 million pounds was lodged in this account at 30 June 1957. In addition, 64.5 million pounds was held in liquid assets and Commonwealth government securities.
>
> Advances showed little change, increasing by 1 million pounds to 106 million pounds. Nevertheless, the volume of repayments received from existing advances made it possible to approve new loans amounting to 26 million pounds.

By contrast, here are a couple of executive job ads that came our way recently. To some extent, we might presume these are deliberately written in a kind of shorthand, encrypted with meaning decipherable by the cognoscenti, so that the wording helps target the ad, by virtue of baffling the rest of us, to its intended, initiated readership. But there's also a fair bit of frankly clumsy syntax and jargoned, inexact diction on display here, most of it the writer's best shot at executive headhunting patois.

> The client is an independent, not-for-profit, public company managed by a Board comprised of a wide range of stakeholder organisations. Operation in the environmental standards area, revenue to their members with licensed products exceeds $1.5 billion. The organisation is facing rapid demand from producers and there is now an urgent need to resource the ongoing success of the program.

'Resource the ongoing success of the program'!?

Here's one in project-management-speak. If words and time are money, and if writing were a project that mattered as much as any other, why would you bother with 'recently' and 'major' in the opening clause; indeed, why would you bother with that clause at all, or not prefer something shorter like 'After reviewing its S&OP processes' (whatever that acronym might mean)? Notice how much jargon, repetition, awkwardness ('understanding ... to each stage' in the second-last sentence) and overwriting ('the ability to demonstrate a leadership style' as opposed to 'leadership that inspires ...') afflict this copy.

> Having recently undertaken a major audit of its S&OP processes, this innovative FMCG organisation has identified significant areas for improvement. As Project Manager you will identify the key deliverables and develop an implementation plan, then drive the required change through the organisation. This will require a detailed understanding and systematic approach to each stage of the S&OP process to ensure full integration. Proven expertise in delivering business process improvement in an FMCG manufacturing or logistics environment is essential, as is the ability to demonstrate a leadership style that inspires confidence and action.

Driving *the required change through the organisation* sounds like fun. And that would be as opposed to driving the kind of change you don't require, we suppose. Copy like this is the antithesis of leadership that inspires confidence and action: how would anyone know what action to take if instructions came in these words?

This ad, by contrast, sticks to details, and uses necessary jargon.

> Managing corporate communications, PR strategy, CEO support (including speeches, presentations, etc), online strategy, collateral and internal communications. This is a diverse marcomms role, requiring someone with superior writing skills, proactive and proven experience in managing end-to-end communications.

The art of the impossible—good writing and competitive edge

Writing suffers because almost everyone writes: because almost everybody writes, it's assumed that almost everybody can. But almost everyone drives, too, and look what happens on the roads.

Few of us are expert; most of us muddle through; and muddling through and making do are about as good as most of us get. Because, in other words, most of us perform something resembling writing every day—whereas we don't put in much time in court, at the white board dreaming up slogans, in Excel doing NPVs, or in the operating theatre performing bypass surgery—most people have trouble seeing writing as a discipline, like law or advertising, accounting or surgery, in which not everyone is equally knowledgeable, well schooled or skilled.

But writing is not a common good; it doesn't come free; and not everyone is equally good at it. Good writers are good from birth, and they get better by practice. They turn up at their drafts the way Kim Clijsters turns up at the practice court, or Usain Bolt at the track, or 'sweet gleaming soprano' Danielle de Niese at voice coaching sessions; they fail again and again, until they start to fail better. The best work hard at doing better what they already do very well.

If you didn't get the writing gene, you can make up for it by getting and following a decent guidebook. And by taking every opportunity you get to write more simply and vividly—practise when nothing turns on it (practise in emails to your friends and colleagues; practise on Twitter) so that you nail it when something does turn on it. But getting any better starts with the recognition that there's something worth getting better at; that there's something to learn; that near enough ain't nearly good enough; that writing is a body of knowledge, not an accident of our being alive in a literate society; that practice makes perfect (or near enough in the long run); that there are standards and devices and hanging offences. Muddling through with writing just won't do. This is language we're talking about here.

And if you don't think you're going to get good enough to write as well as you know you'd like, or as well as the tender or the pitch, the application or the speech deserves—hire someone who can. Hire a writing specialist the way you'd hire a lawyer. Pay them what they're worth—and learn from them, while you're at it.

It was Matthew Gibbs, a professional business communicator and a very fine writer, himself—the one who takes every opportunity to remind us there's no Nobel Prize for business writing—who sparked these last thoughts. He sat at dinner the other night and he spoke out of frustration. Writing doesn't get the respect it deserves at work, he said, because everyone thinks that everyone can write. Worse, lacking an ear for what distinguishes top-drawer writing from copy taken from the middle or bottom drawer, most people don't believe there's much payback for troubling longer—or smarter—over the prose. Like politics, writing is seen as the art of the possible. Compromise is regarded as inevitable; transcendently clear writing, as impossible.

But Matthew's sense is that a little more writing effort can go a very long way; it can yield big returns—returns measurable in increased hits and sales, wider media coverage, stronger brand recognition, enhanced credibility in the market, better pulling power with the kinds of employees you'd like to pull and keep; returns also measurable in how much damage you avoid from customers and regulators and stockholders who don't get to feel baffled, misled or patronised. In Matthew's mind, the returns on a little investment—of faith, time and money—in business writing are reliably strong. And it's the one investment where the risks that give rise to the big returns range from low to non-existent; in fact, the real risk, a guarantee, almost, of negative returns, is the strategy of sticking to the knitting.

Think how much new business a law firm might draw with a website that opens thus:

> Life can seem complex. So can the law. But most things come down to a few simple truths—though you might need some help to find them. If you're in business, you know this. So do we.

On the other hand, this piece of copy might draw more new business if it were more winningly turned and focused on business needs:

> Bishop Wright Paz partners are universally recognised as being leaders across a wide range of legal practice areas.

A quick whip around the big law firms reveals web copy that is almost interchangeable. It's competent but generic. Like this:

> Berger Michaels is an international law firm with more than 1500 people in 16 cities in the Asia Pacific region and expertise across the range of corporate law.
>
> Woods Carey is one of the largest full-service law firms in the Asia Pacific region. With more than 300 partners and 1200 legal staff located in Australia, China, Hong Kong, Indonesia, New Zealand and the UK, Woods Carey supports leading industry and government clients when and where they need us.

'When and where they need us' is good, but 'supports' is one of the most overused, vague and yawn-inducing verbs in the managerial lexicon. It's so overused because, of course, it spares you the trouble of briefly and clearly saying just what it is that you do to help. The convention seems to be to emphasise size, geographic spread, blue-chip cred of clients, and breadth of legal expertise. But if I'm not a blue-chip customer, wouldn't I be scared off? Is this code for 'we charge the highest fees'? And what do I care that you're busy making money in China, if I want you to help me with my defamation matter in Geelong?

This is catchier and more likely to persuade the sceptical:

> Some lawyers focus on resolving issues fast; we think ahead to help prevent issues arising.

This one comes off as hokey, but at least they're trying:

> From a timber cottage in Main Street to new, sleek and ultra-modern offices over fifty years later, Le Favre & Co has firmly cemented itself as one of the leading edge law firms in Lake Jindabyne.

In all these cases, and many others like them, a little more writing and a little less business would do wonders for the business.

The business case—and beyond—for great writing at work

In what's left of this little black book, and by way of coming to some kind of a conclusion, let's make the case for good business writing. Why does good writing matter—for you, for your company, for your research, for your career, for your leadership aspirations, for all of us who have to read the kind of stuff people like you get to write? Let's make the moral and political case for good writing. Let's make the case for beauty over ugliness. Let's show how good writing makes good leadership. But first of all, since this is a book of business writing, let's make the business case for the kind of writing—sound, trim, engaging, humane, graceful—this book has been about.

1 GOOD WRITING IS GOOD BUSINESS

We hope the book has made this case in detail and at length. But here, in three dot points, is the business case for better business writing.

- Good writing is a core business process—communication—performed efficiently. When you write well, you mean the most in the fewest words; you get the most out of the fewest inputs; you waste no one's time or money; you spend that most precious resource, language, wisely, and with it you manufacture sense. If elegant business processes make business sense, elegant writing—the process by which a business makes sense to its customers—makes business sense, too. At least as much sense as, say, elegant logistics and state-of-the-art warehousing.

- The way you write positions you; how you write implies the kind of person, the kind of business, you are. Good writing positions you as careful, intelligent, thoughtful, imaginative, coherent, elegant, capable of thinking for yourself and taking account of the humanity of your readers. It makes you stand out in ways in which it's good to stand out. *How* you tell your story—how engagingly, how trimly, how memorably, how smoothly—is more important than most of the detail you include in it; what it wins you may not be the Nobel Prize, but it may be the degree, the grant, the job, the case, the respect, the market share, the competitive edge.

- Since everyone writes, since business is largely transacted in language, writing well will be a source of competitive advantage. If you write better than your competitors—you make more sense faster and more smoothly than your rivals—you're likely to attract the right kind of attention, and you're likely to attract some business. Maybe a lot. Who wouldn't rather do business or work with someone they understand at pace? (See what Matthew Gibbs had to say about this in the previous section.)

But the business case for better writing is only where the case for good writing begins. There are other reasons to write well. Some for your sake; some for ours—the people, your sometime readers, who share the public space with you.

2 GOOD WRITING IS GOOD IN ITSELF

Good writing is just plain good, the way good health is—good sex, good weather, good soil, good food and wine. Good writing is just inherently good; it shares more meaning fast; it doesn't tax its readers more than it must; it gives them an easy ride to meaning; it may even give them pleasure; at very least, it gives them swiftly back to their real lives, a little wiser, and unworried. If those are not incontrovertible goods, it's hard to say what is. And the goodness of good writing matters because we lead our lives, we tell ourselves who we are, and we come to understand the world, in language, and language is how we relate to each other; so whatever contributes to the health of language contributes to the health of whatever we use it for: to the health, in other words, of society, markets, education, the works.

3 BETTER WRITING MIGHT HELP US IMAGINE AND MAKE A BETTER WORLD

Language constructs reality. How we describe reality is how we experience it. Conventional managerial, bureaucratic and academic language describes a sterile and inarticulate world of inputs and outputs, projects and programs, implementations and initiatives, drivers and deliverables, KPIs and objectives—a world that plays false to the real world, of people and things, we really live and think and trade in. The kind of language so many people feel obliged to use at work offers an impoverished picture of the work they actually do, the thoughts they actually think and the world they actually live in; bad language impoverishes us all.

4 GOOD WRITING SPARES THE WORLD UNNECESSARY UGLINESS

And that has to be another good thing, in itself. Beauty—or at least the absence of ugliness—tends to help things along. This is the aesthetic case for graceful writing. Beauty is sometimes a hard case to make, especially in academic, scientific, engineering and banking circles. Beauty is said to be in the beholder's eye, and that may well be true. But let's agree at least that beauty, some kind of aesthetic good, includes elegance—it is simplicity in perfection; it is the making of only as many gestures as are absolutely essential to perform a given task, making perfect sense, in writing's case. Elegant writing is simply better writing than inelegant writing, unless it is your purpose to infuriate, dissemble or baffle.

5 GOOD WRITING MAKES THE WRITER LOOK GOOD

Just as good writing positions the organisation, it also, perhaps even more so, positions the individual writer. If your writing's much good, you come across as smart and empathetic, original and memorable. If it's longwinded and unsound, awkward and clichéd, you come across as—well, you can work it out. One senior policy maker once told us that he learned to write well out of his deep-seated fear of looking ridiculous. With luck, this book has shown how absurd, how pompous and foolish bad writing sounds; if you don't want to sound like a goose, good writing will serve you well; bad writing, of the conventional kind, will cook you. Trouble is, of course, when pomposity is the norm, it won't seem as absurd to most people as it should; it won't occur to many writers that another kind of writing is possible.

So writing well will spare you embarrassment; you might choose to write better, in other words, out of self-interest—to earn and keep a good reputation. But there are altruistic reasons, too.

6 GOOD WRITING IS GOOD ETHICS

There is an ethics to good writing: good writing is gracious and empathetic; it's good manners. Good writing elevates a reader's needs—the customer, the examiner, the client, the colleague—above one's own. A good writer pursues, as a minimum standard, the golden rule: do unto others as you would have them do unto you. That is, write without any of the awkwardness, evasion and pomposity you hate reading from others. Good writing is essentially empathetic (it imagines the reader's needs and tries to meet them), and empathy is a virtue. A virtue, as it happens, that may also win you the business. Good writing speaks its reader's language—which is the best kind of language to make your case in—the idiom most likely to convince them you know what you mean and that it matters to them.

7 BETTER WRITING MAKES SOCIETIES BETTER

Beyond the service of the individual reader's needs, there is a wider, social ethic that good writing serves. Markets run efficiently and without distortion when vendors and other stakeholders make full and bona fide disclosure of all relevant information; open democracies function best when the voters know whom and what they're voting for—when the press is free and speeches are replete with vivid detail. Everything runs better when we know what we're doing. And good writing—in journalism, policy, legislation, scholarship, contracts, prospectuses, information brochures, textbooks and so on—is the larger part of how we make sure we do. Yet most of the big conversation society shares is conducted in writing of the kind this book has critiqued. The more clearly and elegantly these pieces of functional prose are written, the better society is likely to run: the more we will know, the less wool can be pulled over anyone's eyes, the wiser our decisions are likely to be, at polling booths, kitchen tables, senate hearings and laptops.

8 GOOD WRITING KEEPS MARKETS HONEST AND YOU OUT OF JAIL

Good writing makes markets more efficient and polities more discerning; it adds to the stock of general wisdom. That's the positive moral case for good writing. Put negatively, sloppy writing, writing that doesn't take the trouble to be clear, or writing that overtly dissembles or obfuscates can land you in court, and rightly so. As we write, in the wake of the global financial crisis, court is where a number of financial institutions, and the financial advisers who retailed the institutions' complex products, find themselves. And bad language—sins of commission or omission, perpetrated in prospectuses and sales pitches—is what these lawsuits are about. Big banks and stockbrokers are being sued by investors and chided by regulators and judges, for having failed—at some length and to their own short-term advantage—to make clear the nature of the risk ordinary investors were buying into.

Whatever the legal outcome of such cases, financial institutions, and all of us, are on notice: bad writing won't cut it in the post-GFC world. It's bad manners, it's bad business, it's bad karma, and it's going to bite you on the bottom. Spin is dead in the new era of more exacting and perspicacious regulatory oversight; old-fashioned probity is the new black. So, it might be best these days to work out what you mean, and describe it. Business documents must make sense. Or else.

Poetry, listening and the language of leadership

Good writing will help you manage. It will help you win the deal and get the job and keep it. It will help you gain the edge.

But good writing may also help you lead. In fact, leadership is unimaginable these days without fine writing skills.

Leadership is hard to define, but it has to do with telling the story of who you and your organisation are and where you need to go and how. It has to do with creating and reshaping the vision. Leaders provide clarity—for themselves and their people—about the identity and direction of the enterprise and what makes it stand out. About the work that has yet to be done, and why it must be done and how. Leaders inspire. They persuade and convince and compel. They carry people with them. Leaders show the way. And a good deal of showing the way in business happens in writing.

At very least, a leader will want to make sense; she'll want to demonstrate tidiness of thought. How she writes won't just tell others what she thinks; it will model, in its syntax and diction, in its humanity and clarity, how attentive she is to the picture—big and small. It will show how careful and mindful she is. But if you want to lead, you're going to need to write winningly; you're going to need to sound original. The usual abstractions, the same old empty verbs, the standard-issue managerial or academic diction may convince some that you're not a complete newbie. But they won't galvanise; they won't be good enough to change minds, let alone hearts. For that, you'll need to write—not merely to mimic or conform.

You'll need to make writing that stays written; you'll want to tell a story and offer some turns of phrase that haven't been turned out a million times before. You'll need to sound, in other words, like *someone*, not some disembodied corporate clone, a shirt stuffed with arid and dilapidated clichés—you'll want to sound like someone with a mind of their own and the strength of character, the courage and technique to speak it. And you'll need to know a thing or two about punctuation, poetics and persuasion.

The leader knows, or must learn, what the storyteller and, above all, the poet knows: words—which ones you choose and how you lay them out—have the power to quicken the dead and they have the power, when used with less thought and skill, to deaden the quick. Poets know some things that leaders could do with knowing, too. In his book *The Heart Aroused*, the poet and teacher David Whyte talks about these things. Poets have the gift—they have the linguistic knack—of finding words to speak simply, profoundly and engagingly about deep and universal human experiences. They are the masters of the apt word, the right rhythm and the telling image.

Poets, as Seamus Heaney notes in *The Redress of Poetry*, can't seem to help fronting what are often thought of as the negative aspects, the shadow side, of human behaviour and endeavour, but they do it with equanimity; they manufacture wisdom and a certain kind of grace and beauty, no matter what they have in their sights. Since leaders, too, are going to need to address the challenges and shortcomings as well as the triumphs of the enterprise, they could take a lesson from the poets. Franklin D Roosevelt did: 'We have nothing to fear but fear itself'. Paul Keating did: 'It was we who did the dispossessing. We took the traditional lands and smashed the traditional way of life. We brought the diseases ...' And so, more recently, did Barack Obama: 'Our health care is too costly, our schools fail too many, and each day brings further evidence that the ways we use energy strengthen our adversaries and threaten our planet ... Today I say to you that the challenges we face are many. But this is America. They will be met.'

Good writing helps leaders win and keep the attention of their people, because it speaks to the full person of the reader, to their human nature.

Poetic language squeezes out cant, cliché and empty abstraction; it makes room instead for a little reality in all its human complexity; it helps leaders keep things, or make things, real. And it helps a leader sell and make change, and make it last, because it avoids the usual platitudes, the vacuous tropes—and because, as a result, it sounds powerful and believable.

Poetry changes things because it reaches people deep down, and changes *them*, sometimes for good. There's no turning back for the poet, writes David Whyte; and there's none for his reader either, if the poem is good. At its best a poem seems to speak a kind of truth, a wisdom much greater than anything the writer knows or is stuck on, a wisdom the right language gives one entry to—plainly and profoundly. It says difficult things so beautifully we don't feel we can turn away.

> No man is an island, entire of itself; each is a piece of the continent, a part of the main ... Any man's death diminishes me because I am involved in mankind, and therefore never send to know for whom the bell tolls: it tolls for thee.
>
> —John Donne, 'Meditation XVII'

> O the mind, mind has mountains; cliffs of fall
> Frightful, sheer, no-man fathomed. Hold them cheap
> May who ne'er hung there ...
>
> —Gerard Manley Hopkins, 'No Worst, There is None'

> 'Hope' is the thing with feathers—
> That perches in the soul—
> And sings the tune without the words—
> And never stops—at all—
>
> —Emily Dickinson, '254'

> Tell me about despair, yours, and I will tell you mine.
> Meanwhile the world goes on …
> Meanwhile the wild geese, high in the clean blue air,
> are heading home again.
>
> —Mary Oliver, 'Wild Geese'

> Beauty is truth, truth beauty,—that is all
> Ye know on earth, and all ye need to know.
>
> —John Keats, 'Ode on a Grecian Urn'

> Things fall apart; the centre cannot hold;
> Mere anarchy is loosed upon the world …
> The best lack all conviction, while the worst
> Are full of passionate intensity.
>
> —WB Yeats, 'The Second Coming'

Hear the complex, profound simplicity in these lines ('things fall apart; the centre cannot hold', '"hope" is the thing with feathers'); note the balance ('beauty is truth, truth beauty') and how tidily these propositions are put ('the best lack all conviction', 'that is all ye know on earth, and all ye need to know', 'the mind has mountains', 'no man is an island'); hear how much like talking this is, only better. Much better, but not much different. Hear the rhythm; see the geese, the things with feathers, the falcon; feel the terror and the hope. Next time you feel a cliché coming on, open a book of poems instead; find a website of great quotations and notice how many of them come from poets.

You don't need to become a poet to become a leader—to write the way you'll need to write to lead. But it wouldn't hurt to read some. Poetry could teach a leader, or anyone at work, most of what they need to know about writing as enacted leadership. The point is to practise on your subject matter the kind of care the poet practises on hers—and to master as much of the technique of the poet as you can: the elegant simplicity, the humanity of diction, the shapeliness of phrase, the timing.

A good part of leading well is writing well. Making sense on the page isn't nearly enough, though it would be a start. Telling the truth would also help. But it's not what sense you make and what kind of truth you tell—it's *how*. Write with an ear for your rhythms and sound effects, and favour modes of telling that help your listeners listen and remember. Show; don't tell. Keep your voice active. Favour the concrete over the abstract, the specific over the general, the short over the long; be generous with the truth but economical with the way you tell it; put some people in, including yourself; use some real verbs; tell, above all, a story; don't make it rhyme, but *do* make it swing—rhythm is the ultimate persuader.

This will sound strange, but good writing seems not just to *speak* to its readers and to *tell* them something the writer wants them to know; good writing *listens*. Books and poems and speeches that sway us say things we seem to remember thinking and feeling, ourselves, once. Good writing tells us our own truths—aspects of our own untold stories.

This happens partly because good writing speaks in the diction and rhythms of speech of its readers. And so it feels in some way like our own—a response to a question we might almost have asked. Even if you haven't done much focus-grouping, you're likely to sound as though you're listening, not just talking, the more you adopt the words and phrases people use in conversation. The more human your writing is, the more voice it has, the more it will sound like part of a conversation your reader has been carrying on with you all along.

Writing is, of course, more likely to sound like listening—like the reader's own thoughts trimmed, elevated and returned to them—if the writing really does follow and articulate a process of engaged and active listening. Of dialogue and conversation. For leadership is a reciprocal relationship, and a fair bit of it is about attentiveness and empathy—like writing, indeed. A good part of leadership is active and critical listening; it is the asking of many questions and the acknowledgment of many different answers; the rest of it is thinking straight and framing messages that embrace and interpret and add value to the things your people told you when you attended to them. Good leadership seems to tell an organisation its own story, in language clearer and more precise and engaging than it had managed yet on its own.

In a lecture we attended recently, Fred Greenstein, assessing the presidency of Barack Obama, employed a metric of six 'leadership qualities':

- public communication
- organisational ability
- political skill
- policy vision
- cognitive style
- emotional intelligence.

It struck us that all but two (organisational ability and political skill) of these leadership qualities had a lot to do with writing—or, at least, the skills of mind one employs in writing, as in leading. Writing speeches and all manner of communications is clearly central (Greenstein puts it first) to leadership. 'Policy vision' involves clarity of mind and articulation, and Greenstein used that piece of Obama's inaugural address we quoted earlier to illustrate Obama's gift in this area. Finally, clear thinking ('cognitive style') and mastery of one's emotions ('emotional intelligence') are disciplines a good writer, like a good leader, could use, too.

It turns out, then, that this is a book for leaders, not just for managers and scholars, lawyers and scientists and public servants. The struggle to improve your sentences is not just the struggle to lift your profits or your grades, your ROI, your value-add, or your QA and your service levels; it's the struggle to improve your self, and in the process the calibre of the conversation we all share about our lives and futures.

NOTE ON SOURCES

Since showing works better—and lasts longer—than telling, we've used as many examples in this book as we could find. We've tried to exemplify every point we make, every principle and practice, both good and bad, we discuss, and every kind of document we explore, from emails to proposals.

Though all of our examples are drawn from life, some are composites, some are incredibly lifelike facsimiles, and some are digitally enhanced for ethical or pedagogical reasons. Where we don't give a source, you can assume

- We made it up
- We dressed it up
- We don't think it's wise, or important, to say where we found it, or
- We think we attributed it adequately in the text.

Here then is our selective note on sources.

Page 7: *For each parcel of land*: a local council letter

Page 8: *Refugees and humanitarian clients*: (Australian federal) Department of Immigration and Citizenship (DIAC), a strategic plan for identity management, *Identity Matters*

Page 8: *On the question*: an academic's response to queries on a grant application

Page 8: *The organisational change programme*: DIAC, *Identity Matters*

Page 8: *The government is committed*: a federal government minister in a press release

Page 19: *No one can possibly know*: Robert Solow, "How to Understand the Disaster", *The New York Review of Books*, 14 May 2009

Page 19: *Let's think about organizations*: Gareth Morgan, *Images of Organization*

Page 20: *But this theory can be tested*: *The Origin of Species*

Page 20: *So if we rule out an EFT*: the blog of Malcolm Turnbull MP

Page 21: *This document outlines*: PA Consulting tender document

Page 21: *You'll need to complete this form*: accountant for a US publishing house

Page 21: *'Family Settings'*: Microsoft Australia

Page 24: *John Maynard Keynes*: letter to the editor, *Australian Financial Review*

Page 24: *With six of the top-10*: letter to the editor, *The Sydney Morning Herald*

Page 24: *If it is the first step*: "I Clip, Therefore I Am", *Sydney Alumni Magazine*

Page 25: *ASX believes the timeframe*: quoted in an article in *The Sydney Morning Herald*

Page 31: *The confluence of many factors*: Rajni Mala, Macquarie University

Page 38: *Virgin Green Fund*: the Virgin Green Fund website

Page 39: *Global warming is caused*: Mark Maslin, *Global Warming: A Very Short Introduction*

Page 42 *A simple recipe for working women*: Jack Vaughan, ad copy for AMLC

Page 42: *The policy tools exist*: *The Stern Review: The Economics of Climate Change*

Page 42: *The Great Inflection*: Thomas

Friedman, *The New York Times*, 12 December 2009

Page 42: *The last few decades have belonged*: Daniel Pink, *A Whole New Mind*

Page 44: *Remy Martin Luis XIII*: Jack Vaughan, ad copy for Vintage Cellars

Page 44: *In the late Cretaceous*: John McPhee, *Rising from the Plains*

Page 44: *In 2004, when Google*: www.google.org

Page 52: *The transition to a low-carbon economy*: *The Stern Review*

Page 52: *Timely warnings save lives*: *Interim Report of the 2009 Victorian Bushfire Royal Commission*

Page 52: *Discontinuous change requires discontinuous thinking*: Charles Handy, *The Age of Unreason*

Page 53: *He was an old man who fished alone*: Ernest Hemingway, *The Old Man and the Sea*

Page 59: *What a piece of work is man*: William Shakespeare, *Hamlet*

Page 59: *All good things come by grace*: Norman Maclean, *A River Runs Through It*

Page 59: *Read a few pages of Emily Dickinson*: John Berger, *Hold Everything Dear*

Page 59: *We must return to our bodies*: Octavio Paz, *The Double Flame*

Page 61: *Regardless of the particular data quality issue*: The Australian National Audit Office (ANAO), report 28, 2008–09

Page 63: *Divorce may be the end of a marriage*: New Zealand Ministry of Justice, *Parenting Plans: Parents' Guide to Making Plans for their Children after Separation*

Page 64: *Until 30 June, the government is virtually giving money away*: Jack Vaughan, ad copy for Perpetual

Page 64: *It doesn't last forever*: Jack Vaughan, ad copy for Hyundai

Page 66: *The cause of URTI*: National Prescribing Service, guidelines booklet

Page 71: *India has certain advantages*: Michael Wood, *The Story of India*

Page 74: *Many critics believe*: a finance scholar

Page 74: *We deliver what we promise*: a courier company

Page 75: *This study looks at the complexities*: Gordon Mills, abstract for a seminar, "Competition and Collusion in Short-haul Airline Markets"

Page 76: *The need to clearly establish identity*: DIAC, *Identity Matters*

Page 78: *This strategic plan articulates the business need*: DIAC, *Identity Matters*

Page 78: *The PDRs reveal*: Department of Families, Housing, Community Services and Indigenous Affairs, *Strategic Indigenous Housing and Infrastructure Program—Review of Program Performance*, August 2009

Page 79: *The capital works funding*: *Strategic Indigenous Housing and Infrastructure Program*

Page 79: *We need out performance*: ANZ, Annual Report 2008

Page 81: *Women, during pregnancy*: Jack Vaughan, ad copy for AMLC

Page 81: *With no change*: Lenore Taylor, *The Weekend Australian*, 28–29 November 2009

Page 81: *Tax expenditures*: ANAO, report 32, 2007–08

Page 81: *In 2006–07, tax expenditures*: ANAO, report 32, 2007–08

Page 82: *As noted in Section 2.6*: Director of National Parks, *Uluru–Kata Tjuta National Park Plan of Management 2010–20*

Page 83: *Compared to outlays*: ANAO, report 32, 2007–08

Page 84: *The right vehicle*: David Morris, ad copy for Land Rover

Page 84: *To complete this quote*: NRMA Insurance website

Page 84: *The only disappointment*: Jack Vaughan, ad copy for Maserati

Page 84: *Spring reaches the summit*: Jack Vaughan, ad copy for Thredbo

Page 84: *If you're planning to have treatment*: MBF Health/NRMA Insurance brochure

Page 86: *The department anticipates that the key deliverables*: DIAC, *Identity Matters*

Page 97: This model is adapted from Edward

Bailey, *Plain English at Work*

Page 114: *The Movement Alert List*: Australian National Audit Office, Report No 35, 2008–09

Page 117: *What you call great music*: a radio station's mission statement

Page 117: *Researchers have found*: an item on the television news

Page 118: *The report that follows*: ANAO, report 25, 2008–09

Page 119: *The Australian Government has a large environmental footprint*: this is Mark's reworking of the summary; the text is different in the published report

Page 120: *This audit reviews*: Again, this is Mark's reworking of the executive summary to the published audit report

Page 120: The headings: ANAO, report 35, 2008–09

Page 121: *Bank failures come in waves*: We've tidied this a little, but it was always well written, and its author deserves mention for that: Shauna Ferris of Macquarie University

Page 121: *Prior to 7 February*: *Interim Report of the 2009 Victorian Bushfire Royal Commission*

Page 130: *Banks, the regulator and Storm*: *The Sydney Morning Herald*, 6 November 2009

Page 160: *Study highlights*: Medscape, 30 November 2009

Page 161: *Ethics at Work*: Advertising Federation of Australia, St James Ethics Centre and David Morris

Page 188: *Our research shows*: policy document, the National Prescribing Service

Page 188: *In May 2008*: a young accounting academic

Page 188: *We deliver*: a courier company

Page 200: *I once saw a hospital discharge diagnosis*: Robert Solow, "How to Understand the Disaster", *The New York Review of Books*, 14 May 2009

Page 202: *During 1956–57 total assets rose*: The Commonwealth Bank of Australia

Page 206: *Life can seem complex*: Till Henderson Lawyers, New Zealand

Page 218: see Fred Greenstein, *The Presidential Difference*, 2009

INDEX